COME,
LORD JESUS

COME, LORD JESUS

Meditations on the Art of Waiting

MOTHER MARY FRANCIS, P.C.C.

IGNATIUS PRESS   SAN FRANCISCO

Cover art:
Bartolomé Esteban Murillo
The Holy Family
Erich Lessing / ArtResource, New York

Cover design by Riz Boncan Marsella

© 2010 by Ignatius Press, San Francisco
All rights reserved.
ISBN 978-1-58617-480-4
Library of Congress Control Number 2010922763
Printed in the United States of America ⦾

DEDICATED TO

HIS HOLINESS POPE BENEDICT XVI

WHO

BY THE RADIANT CLARITY OF HIS TEACHING

AND

THE LUMINOUS EXAMPLE OF HIS GOODNESS

TIRELESSLY PREPARES THE CHURCH

FOR

THE COMING OF THE LORD JESUS

CONTENTS

Foreword 9

FIRST WEEK OF ADVENT

Introduction	*Folded Wings*	15
First Sunday (YEAR A)	*Plowshares*	19
First Sunday (YEAR B)	*A Heart on Tiptoe*	22
First Sunday (YEAR C)	*The Path*	26
Monday	*Rush Out to Meet Him*	32
Tuesday	*Wonder*	36
Wednesday	*Right Nutrition*	40
Thursday	*The Epicenter*	45
Friday	*A Pattern of Giving*	49
Saturday	*Knowing the Need to Be Forgiven*	55

SECOND WEEK OF ADVENT

Second Sunday (YEAR A)	*Giving Evidence*	65
Second Sunday (YEAR B)	*God's Mercy and Love*	69
Second Sunday (YEAR C)	*Silence before the Lord God*	73
December 8	*A Cleaned Heart*	77
December 12	*Golden Rocks*	82
Monday	*Faith, Hope, and Love*	86
Tuesday	*Wide Open Gates*	90
Wednesday	*Advent Overflow*	93
Thursday	*Great Moments*	98
Friday	*Happy Struggles*	101
Saturday	*The Joy of Being Forgiven*	105

THIRD WEEK OF ADVENT

Third Sunday (YEAR A)	*True Rejoicing*	113
Third Sunday (YEAR B)	*Joyous Replies*	120
Third Sunday (YEAR C)	*Happenings*	126
Monday	*Companionship*	131
Tuesday	*Joyful Penitence*	135
Wednesday	*Jubilant Rejection*	139
Thursday	*Success*	147
Friday	*High Ambition*	153
Saturday	*[See December 17, or appropriate day]*	

FOURTH WEEK OF ADVENT

Fourth Sunday (YEAR A)   *The Armor of Light*   161

Fourth Sunday (YEAR B)   *The Highly Favored One*   167

Fourth Sunday (YEAR C)   *Great Expectations*   174

CHRISTMAS NOVENA:

December 17   *Waiting*   181

December 18   *Lift Up Your Heads and See*   187

December 19   *The Service of His Plan*   192

December 20   *A Love-Watch*   201

December 21   *A Welcome Sound*   204

December 22   *Love beyond All Telling*   209

December 23   *The Blueprint of Each Day*   213

December 24   *The Kindness and Love of God*   219

FOREWORD

In the fall of 2003, when Mother Mary Francis was waiting at the Chicago airport for her return flight to Roswell after the completion of a visitation to our youngest daughter-house, she began her new book on Advent in the following words:

THE ART OF WAITING

1. Waiting as a child
2. Waiting in fear
3. Waiting in joyous expectation
4. Waiting in peace
5. Waiting to understand
6. Waiting in airports
7. Waiting to see the Face of God

There is this about waiting: it is multifaceted. We can wait in fear. We can wait in joyous expectation. We can be content to wait to be understood when God strikes the moment rather than trying to turn the clock, the calendar, ahead to our preferred moment of "now!" We can stand patiently or irritably in line at the airport. We can wait with the deliciousness of a child's waiting for Christmas. We can wait in peace for God to strike his own moment, reveal his own plans, unveil the demands of his love. And we can see all life and its often bewildering hours and events as a waiting to see the Face of God, which vision is less the explanation of life on earth than a revelation of the mystery of his love. It is ours to determine how to wait. And Advent dawns upon our hearts and souls each year to educate us in the art, the bliss, the peace, the pain, and the wonder of waiting.

It is our Lady who shows us how to wait.

There are two species of humanity as regards reading a book: those who begin reading on page one and arrive eventually at the final page, and those who must read the end before reading what precedes and leads to the end. All of us belong to a crossed species, even our Lady. The foremost handmaid of the Lord wanted some details, some explanation of God's doings. "Behold, I am the handmaid of the Lord." But also: "How shall this be done? I know not man." And the angel's reply was hardly something to answer the human question satisfactorily. "The Holy Spirit shall come upon thee." But who is the Holy Spirit? "And the Holy to be born of you shall be called the Son of God." These are scarcely explanations that would have elicited a reply of: "Oh, I see." No, she did not see.

"Be it done to me according to your word." But how will this word function, so to speak? Blessedly comforting for us are those words of Scripture: "She did not understand." Not then, nor later, either. Gently upbraiding her boy, who was the Son of God, she was later to exercise her maternal rights by asking: "Why have you done this?" when he had been missing for three days in the temple. The reply of the Divine Child was hardly an explanation. "Did you not know that I must be about my Father's business?" What business? But we do not find her presenting more questions. "She did not understand this word that he spoke to her." So, she just went home and cooked supper for him and Saint Joseph.

Alas, because her notes were set aside for "later", this was as far as the new book had progressed before the Great Advent of the Lord in Mother's own life. He came for her on February 11, 2006, unveiling all the mysteries of the Gospel that she pondered in the passage above. We, her spiritual daughters, were left with a great legacy in the conferences Mother gave to our community during her forty-two years as abbess. She had planned to edit her conferences for Advent into a book; but the Lord changed her plans, as he had so often done before.

Eager to share the treasures she poured out upon us, we feel impelled to make them available to a wider audience. Mother did not give an orderly commentary on the Scripture readings of each day of Advent but spoke to us on whatever subject our Lord put into her heart as certain passages in the liturgy struck her. She would often reflect on the Sunday readings; for the rest, her chapters explored any of the other multitudinous facets of Advent, touching on a number of passages more than once and opening out new vistas of meaning each time. As a wise spiritual guide, Mother knew that repetition is indispensable in teaching, and it was also an element of her literary style.

We have gathered together her Advent conferences given from 1967 to 2001 and spread the rich viands of her thoughts over the course of the season, striving to match the daily Mass readings as far as possible. May these ponderings of Mother Mary Francis' heart help each reader to learn more fully the art, the bliss, the peace, the pain, and the wonder of waiting!

The Poor Clare Nuns

MONASTERY OF OUR LADY OF GUADALUPE
ROSWELL, NEW MEXICO
DECEMBER 12
SOLEMNITY OF OUR LADY OF GUADALUPE

FIRST WEEK OF ADVENT

First Sunday of Advent

Introduction: Folded Wings

First Lesson at Matins

I AM quite confident all of us have a deep sense of expectation, joy, and wonderment that Advent is about to begin. We look at the different facets of this season, turning it like a jewel in our hands. Certainly it is a season for children. It is a season of the child, the joy of the Child who came to give joy to the world. It is a season, certainly, of the family, of the community. Family life was solidly established in a lowly, humble, poor place, with three persons who loved utterly and were utterly given— even the Child, from the first moment, because he was divine. It is a season of great tenderness, and a season of hush. It is a season for everyone. It is a season particularly of the woman. It is the woman, especially the religious woman, who has great potential for the spiritual maternity which was so basic in our Lady and which was ratified on Calvary when she became the Mother of all the redeemed: "Woman, behold your son." It is a precious season. Advent summons us to fold the wings of our souls. There is rich meaning in the expression "folded wings". Wings that remain always folded and are never spread to fly in giving would be wings that would deteriorate in atrophy, whereas wings that are always spread and never folded in intense personal prayer, reflection, contemplation would be wings quickly spent or, perhaps, misspent. With all of this—the joy, the tenderness, the maternal

sense, the deepening of womanhood, the folded wings—
Advent is a season of tremendous purpose.

Our Mother the Church is happy as she begins her
Office, and in the first antiphon of Vespers she says, "Pro-
claim the good news!" Then, in her second antiphon, as
though going on to explain to her eager children, she says,
"Know that the Lord is coming." In the third, she says
what is explicated so well in the readings from Isaiah:
"The Lord will come with mighty power." He is coming
to give that power and expecting it to be used.

Holy Mother Church finds no need to modulate into a
different key when, after having made these joyous, wondrous announcements, she says in her first reading at Matins, "Cease doing evil." She is not saying, "Well, it is a
season of tenderness, and I am going to sing you lullaby
after lullaby. It is a season of joy and nothing must mar it;
there must not be any suffering; no effort is required."
"Cease doing evil", she says, just like that! "And learn to
do good"—there is work to be done. It is a season of
training, of learning to do good.

In the book of Isaiah, God is telling us just how he feels
about people who have lots of words and don't change
their way of living. There are two phrases I would like to
pick out especially. When God says, "Bring no more
worthless offerings", how does this apply to us? What is a
worthless offering? I think it is something that costs us
nothing and we pretend it is a gift. We have that other
word of Scripture which is so very precious to me: "I will
not offer the Lord God sacrifices that cost me nothing"
(2 Sam 24:24). In other words, a worthless offering is a
sacrifice that costs me nothing. I am very sweet and agreeable because nothing is disturbing me. I am very charitable
because no one is crossing me. I am very serene and amen-

able and amicable because no one is disturbing me. I am very prayerful because no one is bothering me. All of these delusions are worthless offerings, sacrifices that cost me nothing. Nothing.

We have a very good check on how prayerful we are when there are some disturbances about; we see what our charity is when a bit of stress is put upon it; we see just how sweet we are when someone crosses us; we see how patient we are when things do not go as we had expected and predicted.

Then God has another word about "octaves with wickedness". We think, "Well, what would that have to do with us?" Everything; or the Church would say, Skip this paragraph; this has nothing to do with you. She doesn't do that. I think it is obvious that "octaves with wickedness" means the same thing as "worthless offerings": no action at all. Wickedness does not at all necessarily imply gross sin, but it is doing nothing.

Have we gone from week to week in the wickedness of not changing? Perhaps I must say that in the spiritual life I am as demanding as ever, as complaining as ever, as immature as ever, as impatient as ever—this entire dreary list that we know so well. I think this is very precisely what it means and it has everything to do with us. "Bring no more worthless offerings." Let us reply with a resounding, "No, I won't. I'm not going to bring you any more worthless offerings, sacrifices that cost me nothing. I am not going to celebrate any more octaves with the wickedness of doing nothing, of failing to incarnate in my life the points, the principles, the inspirations that I find pleasant to hear but make little or no effort to incarnate in my life."

Then, in the way of a mother, after saying these stern words, the Church says in the responsory: "Come, now, let us set things right." So that after her sternest words, which were prefaced by a great call to joy, she doesn't say to any of us, "You are hopeless." She says, "Come, now, let us set things right." So, let us enter into Advent with that spirit: let us set things right. And if we see in our prayer that there is a great deal to set right, we will be very happy. I will be so busy this Advent that I won't have time to get into trouble; I won't have time to bring any worthless offerings; I won't have time to celebrate any wicked octaves. I have so much to do. Let us take this mind of our Mother the Church for our own.

FIRST SUNDAY OF ADVENT, YEAR A

Plowshares

IN ONLY a day we will enter into Advent, this great season of sweetness, of tenderness, of opportunity. I think all of our hearts beat a little faster when we come to another new Church year. Assuredly it is every Christian's season, every Catholic's season. But there is a particular sense in which it is a woman's season. So, we want to become more womanly in this season.

When we come to those familiar passages from Scripture that we have each and every year in Advent, one might think that these are rather dour warnings as we enter into a season of tenderness; but it is not so. The most loving parent, the most loving superior, the most loving bishop—all warn, "Do not go that way. Remember the right way." They warn. So, in the second reading at Holy Mass from Saint Paul we have quite a rousing summons which one could paraphrase in everyday ordinary language as saying, "For heaven's sake, get up! The time is here. This is the time of grace. Don't continue on your old sleepy way. Wake up!" As we would say colloquially, "Wake up and live!" This is the time to grow as the Son of God is growing in the womb of his Mother. This is the time for us to grow, too, in life and in grace. Wake up, the time is at hand!

In the Gospel, our dear Lord is saying very serious words about death, about the end of time. Paul says, "Now is the time." And Jesus says: "There is another time. You don't know what hour or what minute it will be. Be ready." Both of them are saying this, our Redeemer and his commissioned scribe.

So, what are we to do now? We have to remember that we don't know how much time we have. We return to the first reading from Isaiah in which he tells us just what to do. True, he is speaking of nations; he is giving a cosmic direction; but, perhaps even more particularly, he is speaking to us individually; he is speaking to souls. The prophet says, "Turn your swords into plowshares and your spears into pruning hooks." Looking at the terrible things happening throughout the world, we think that this cannot be possible, that human beings could not have come to such a pass, and yet it is true; we see nations divided, fighting perhaps more ferociously than ever, one against the other, nation against nation; and within the community of a nation, one group against another. Swords are being used very abundantly. But one does not see these people using plowshares upon themselves to change their own lives. Instead, their many spears are being jabbed into the heart of humanity, the heart of their fellow men. One does not see them using pruning hooks upon themselves.

For us, what is the application? Surely you hardly need me to elucidate it: that if we are not using the "blades", that are in the power of us all as plowshares to plow up the field of our own interior so that God's grace does not come upon hard lumps of pride, upon hard clods of self-opinionatedness or all of that terrible company, those blades will be used for something else. They will be used for swords: swords of division, swords of pain, swords of criticism, swords of blame. We all have blades (and they are God-given), which are our strength and our power. And each one decides: whether I will strike out with the sword or whether I will turn my sword into a plowshare to plow up my own little heart, getting all hardness out of it—all the hardness out of my spirit, of my soul—and become rich soil for God's planting. He wants so much to plant; He wants us to flower; he wants us to bring forth fruit. But he leaves it to us to work with the plowshare of grace.

There is the other figure: the spears turned into pruning hooks. The spear is a terrible thing. We think immediately of the spear that went so cruelly into the Heart of the dead Redeemer. It is such a cruel thing; it is always pushed forth with great force. Yet, that spear can be bent into a pruning hook to cut off in ourselves what does not belong in a spiritual life, what does not belong in the heart of a Christian.

So, let us go forward together into this so tender, so sweet, and so demanding season, when our dear little all-powerful Redeemer wants to see a plowed-up heart, plowed-up spirit, with no hard clods of pride; but instead someone who has turned her swords into a plowshare upon herself; someone who has turned the spear into a pruning hook and is not depressed or discouraged, but is happy about what she will see, as everyone sees who sets out with a pruning hook: how much there is to be pruned and that there is no time to be lost. This, I think, is what it means to live Advent. It is helpful to read the familiar readings of this First Sunday of Advent backward: Jesus is warning; Paul is saying, "Right now!"; and Isaiah is telling us just what to do.

✣ ✣ ✣ ✣

FIRST SUNDAY OF ADVENT, YEAR B

A Heart on Tiptoe

As I LOOKED over the liturgy of the first Sunday of Advent, I became a bit dizzy with the sweetness of it, the richness of it, the tenderness of it, and the power of it. Every year I love to repeat what is so deep in my heart—that this is the woman's season. Yes, we will share it with all the Church. Yet, in a very particular sense, it is a woman's season. It is a season of burgeoning life, a season of tending life, and a season of becoming.

This is perhaps the greatest theological thunderclap of Advent: that God, who *is*, who only *is*—who has no *was*, who has no *will be*—now, in the Incarnation, is *becoming*. God is doing something that, as God, he could not do: he could not change, he could not grow, he could not become. He simply *is* essence. He is the "is-ness" that is the heart of being. Now, choosing to become incarnate, God, as man, can *become*. During the Advent season we commemorate his *becoming* in the womb of a woman. This season of God's *becoming* is something that we women religious understand in a very particular way, for we have not left our womanhood, our maternity, behind us as we were called to this blessed vocation.

I love to recall the word of the poet Sister Madeleva that I find ineffably dear: "In Advent I always feel that I should walk on tiptoe." Indeed, in the wonder of Advent, we should spiritually walk on tiptoe, full of expectancy, full of wonder.

There is a great movement in our time toward conservation. When it is kept intelligent, it is very, very good. There is a movement against waste; the ecologists are rising up to point out to us how we are wasting creation, we are wasting the atmosphere, or we are wasting the forests. There is, among more people all the time, a sense of the horror of the waste of food, of the waste of life. But the common denominator of all this wastefulness is the waste of grace. Our Lady is the only one who in her complete sinlessness never wasted grace.

This, I believe, should be our goal this Advent: that we will not waste grace. Great things are put before us. The Church becomes, even in her tenderness, very dramatic. "Wake up!" she says. And she will say this again and again in Advent: "Get up out of this torpor, this stupor. Wake up! Now is the time to rise from the spiritual sleepiness, the same old dreary infidelities, the same wastefulness, the same old idling paths, the same old petty self-indulgences. Wake up!" she says.

The incarnate Word came to deliver us from the old slavery of sin. We all know how our faults enslave us. We know how we are committed (in a very dark kind of commitment) to our impatience, to our self-will, to our unwillingness to bear with one another's idiosyncrasies and failings. And certainly we have all had the unhappy experience many times of how these things leave a very bitter taste in our mouths. When we give vent to our impatience, when we show our displeasure with one another, when we strive to get our own way, we know how very quickly this turns to the bitterest of ashes in our mouths. We never have any lasting satisfaction from these things, and sometimes we have not even momentary satisfaction—we are unhappy in the very act of committing the fault. And if getting our way does bring us some momentary satisfaction, we know how evanescent it is, how very quickly it goes, and the bitterness it leaves. This is what Christ came to deliver us from; he came to fill in the valleys in us and to lower the mountains in us. But he can't do this unless we are aware that there are mountains to be leveled, that there are valleys to be filled. The way to be sure of never attaining this awareness would be to fasten our gaze on the valleys of deficiencies or the mountains of faults in others.

So, let us not be foolish; let us work with our Redeemer to fill in the valleys of our own deficiencies and to level the mountains in ourselves because we all have very tall mountains, taller than we know. We are not able to recognize their height yet. But the holier we become and the more we cooperate with grace, the more we are aware of our deficiencies and of the mountainous faults within us. When we do arrive at this stage, we are so occupied with the valleys to be filled and the mountains to be lowered in ourselves, that, *ipso facto*, by a kind of happy reflex, we find no mountains in others; we haven't the time to look for them. We haven't the time or the taste to comment on possible valleys of deficiencies in others. Let us love to dwell on this.

I would suggest that in your prayer you make a little questionnaire of the wonderful antiphons holy Church puts before us. They thrill us. The liturgy is always, in one way or another, saying, "What are you doing about this?" We hear that God is coming with power. Will we let him use that power? God is coming to cleanse our hearts. Will we let him cleanse them? We have that feeling that everything is going to be better; everything is going to turn out all right. Yes, if we will allow it. Will we allow it? At Matins we were told rousingly, "Let us cleanse our hearts for the coming of our great King." What needs scrubbing up? Will we not find that we have to use God's grace to grapple with this fault, this weakness? Cleansing is sometimes an abrasive thing; it hurts. You have to scrub and scrub, or scratch and scratch at a thing. We think of the things that we do to the utensils in the kitchen, in the bake-room. If they were sentient, I think they would say, "Stop that!" They don't want to be treated like that. That is what our poor little weak hearts do; we want God to stop. And that is the subject about which we want to question ourselves in prayer. This season, fraught with grace, is opening out before us. We will not be the same at its close as we are now; we will be different. It is up to each one of us which way the difference will be. It is a season of great adventure, and, yes, the heart should walk on tiptoe, for it is a season of wonder.

❖ ❖ ❖ ❖

FIRST SUNDAY OF ADVENT, YEAR C

The Path

MY DEAR SISTERS, as we come from the glory, the splendor, the gorgeousness of the solemnity of Christ the King and enter through a very low door, under a very humble lintel into Advent, we recognize with wonder that it is the same King who is coming in very lowly form. So, too, each of our lives, and the community life, is one mystery. It is in our lowliness of heart, our poorness, the actuation of our understanding that we are the little poor ones of the Lord that we achieve the greatness for which God has destined us, and in no other way.

What I want to speak about today is the path. A few days ago in the Office (Wednesday Matins, 34th Week Ordinary Time) we had a homily of Saint Macarius, who said, "Woe, woe to the path that is not walked upon." I found that very intriguing. I thought, doesn't he mean, "Woe to the person who does not walk upon the right path"? But no, he is saying woe to the path that is not walked upon. As I pondered this in prayer it became very clear. Woe indeed to the path that is not walked upon because it disappears and there is no longer a visible path. If it is not trodden upon day after day, and preferably by many feet all going that same way, then it loses its firmness and the weeds spring up. Soon it will lose its outline, and after not too long an interval one won't be able to see the path anymore. One could cry out, as though the path itself were a sentient thing, "Oh, woe to the path." It is certainly true, woe to those who have not walked on this right path to God, this path made so clear for us in the holy Gospel. But, also, woe to the path. One can say it in a child's way, "Oh, poor path. You aren't there anymore."

Does this not explain so much that is happening in our time? It is not so much that, after a while, persons say, "Yes, that is the path, all right. But I am going another way." But is it not rather that, if we have not walked that same path all the time, each one and the community together, after a while the path becomes very unclear? And after a while it can't be seen at all. So, we can, in our own individual life, or in a community's life, be going, as we would say colloquially, every which way, because the path is no longer that clearly visible for the simple reason that it is not trodden on day after day.

We certainly must speak about the liturgy of the first Sunday of Advent, and how the path relates to the readings of the Sunday eucharistic liturgy. I must say, I was not too surprised to find it relates very well. It is there in all of them.

Jeremiah, in the first reading, tells us about what is going to happen. A path is taking us somewhere; a path always leads us to a destination. He says, "The days are coming . . ." The end of the path is a little closer than it was last year—maybe for some of us much closer than it was last year. He says, "I will fulfill the promise I made, and I will raise up for David a just shoot; he shall do what is right and just in the land." How do we respond to that? For in our lives, there should always be a response, a kind of responsorial psalm, to the readings that are given to us. The Church says thus and so to us through the Scriptures, and our reception of that living Word of God must answer thus and so. A call is not completed until it is answered. One may say in a certain way the Word of God given us in the liturgy is not complete until it is responded to.

So, when Jeremiah says that the promised one will do what is right and just before the Lord in the land, then our responsory is to walk the path: the path that the Gospel has marked out for us so clearly that sometimes we really can't believe it. We can't quite believe that if we just consistently, constantly, love God and love one another we have fulfilled the whole law. Then we begin to ponder this and we see that, yes, this is very exacting, and we begin to see that the reason we don't fulfill the law is because of the many ways and the many times in which we do not love or do not love enough.

We respond to the reading from Jeremiah that we will do what is right and just, that we will walk on the path, and that there will not be patches of weeds springing up because of our *not* walking on it, but that it will be a trodden path, clearer all the time. You know how, even on wood, repeated steps all going the same way will make beautiful little grooves. Even as a very young girl in our high school, I used to look at the stairs with such love and think what tales they had to tell because there were little foot grooves in all of them from young feet always going the same way. Those were wonderful stairs, and they had come—through the continued following on that path of many, many young persons—to be able to say themselves, "This way, right this way." This is what we must do in community: tread that path of the Gospel life. Nobody has to hold her head and try to figure out what this could possibly mean. It is so clear. So we keep going on that path, and the more we walk on it, generation after generation, the more the path is clearly saying, "Right this way. There are weeds to this side, there is underbrush on that side, there may be poisonous reptiles on that other side; but not on *this* path, this straight path. There are no weeds; there is no underbrush, no undergrowth."

In the second reading, from Thessalonians, Saint Paul tells us to increase in love. He exhorts us never to say, "Well, now I have really done it." In this passage he prays that God will make us overflow with love. When a receptacle is brimful it cannot be moved without spilling. That is the way we should be: spilling over love, overflowing with it. We cannot be at our work without spilling love all over the place; we cannot be at prayer in choir without spilling love; we cannot be at recreation without splashing love all over everybody. Saint Paul says that we should overflow with love for one another. He doesn't just say to overflow with love for God, because it would be a great delusion to think we could overflow with love for God and not overflow with love for one another.

Just a few days ago we were considering together the helpfulness of inverting the Scriptures to return them to God in a different sense, a spousal sense. And so we can take Lucifer's terrible words, "I will be like God", saying in a different mode with complete truth and amazing profundity, "I will be like God. I will be all love." This is God's name. God is love. This is what is revealed to us in the Scriptures. How wonderful it is, that he has told us what is his very essence, his very name. He is love. This is the only way in which we can be like him. We cannot be like him in his other attributes: we cannot be omnipotent, we cannot be omniscient, we cannot be any of those things. But we can love. And we can come by loving to be all love. Then we can say with wonder and with joy, "I will be like God. I will be all love."

Saint Paul is saying, "Walk on this path, this straight Gospel path." Walk on it with a blameless heart, a heart that does not blame, a holy heart that is like God because it is loving all the time. And when it has failed in love in the least measure or in the slightest occasion, it makes reparation. So, dearest sisters, that tells us something about the path.

And then Saint Luke in his Gospel tells us about the last days. In the Gospel about the final days, Saint Luke says men "will die of fright in anticipation of what is coming". We want to stop right there and ask, "Why would we die of anticipation, since we know where this path ends?" Before the revelation of the New Testament, they didn't know. But we do know.

A childhood memory comes to my mind as I say that. My mother had this little idiosyncrasy of always wanting to see how the book ended. When she began to read, she would always read the end, and then she would diligently go back to the beginning and read the book through. It used to amuse me as a child, and I started to do the same thing because you always like to do what your mother does. We want to see how it is going to turn out. And we do know. We know what is at the end of the path. And so, if we die of anticipation, we should be dying of joy, dear sisters. When we are not anticipating rightly because we are not going firmly forward on the path, is it not because we are anticipating lesser things? I listed some of them here: What do we anticipate? Do we waste our energy sometimes on anticipating how it is going to turn out? We think: things are going to get worse and worse, and I don't think I can do this, and I don't think I can make that much effort, and maybe it won't come out right anyway, and I'd better not do it at all because maybe I can't—and so I excuse myself from effort. This is what we do. We anticipate the wrong things. Why do we not anticipate the best things? Because even in the things that cause us the most suffering, God always has in mind something wonderful for which we need to be purified by suffering. And so we know where the path ends.

Just today we had a message from a community in Texas where one of the elderly sisters died at the age of ninety-five, very bright, very clear. As she was being taken by ambulance to the hospital she said three different times, "Oh, Jesus, I'm so eager to see you." This is real anticipation. This is someone who had really been walking on the path and knew what was at the end. And now she was saying, "It's almost here. I'm so eager to see you."

So, dearest sisters, that is my Advent word for you, for myself, about the path. It can become indistinct; it can be lost, so that we can think that we are walking on the path when we no longer are. It can lose its great functionality, which is to lead us straight forward. This Advent path now leads straight to Bethlehem. We certainly don't want to make any detours. We want to help one another keep on the path. Sometimes, as happens to all of us, we wander off in our weakness from the path, but when we see which way the others are going, we will hurry back to be with them. When we wander off in these worldly cares, there isn't any peace, and we become very unlovable to live with because we are not at peace. Peace is on the path.

✣   ✣   ✣   ✣

Rush Out to Meet Him

AS WE BEGIN this Advent season, we have a tender yearning for the coming of Christ in the Parousia, a desire to bring forth Christ in our souls, and a great sense of comradeship with our Blessed Mother. During her weeks and months of waiting, she waited in much the same context as we live our lives; she spent those sacred weeks and months doing much the same type of thing that we do. And yet this tenderness must bring forth something great in us; this tenderness must have about it a very resolute character. The Church is very successful, as she invariably is, in blending these two elements in her liturgy. She expresses her tenderness for the coming little Lord of heaven and earth. At the same time, she speaks in resounding words of this coming Redeemer and his greatness. She wants us to yearn, but not in any kind of supine way. There is nothing restful about Advent yearning.

For instance, the Office says, "Let us cast off deeds of darkness." Each one has to discover in prayer, by the light of the Holy Spirit, what her works of darkness are. If we do not lead a deeply prayerful, recollected life, then it is possible—and this is tragic—not to discover what our own works of darkness are. And the second part of this tragedy is that, by never discovering what our own works of darkness are, we can become very adept at seeing what we think are works of darkness in others. One point I would like to make in regard to this concept is that we must all be careful that we are not vexed at supposed faults in others, which are really caused, are projected, by one's own works of darkness. I think this bears a lot of looking into. We should be very alert for the things in ourselves that evoke unpleasant responses in others. When we are distressed at someone else's response or some supposed deficiency in her behavior, let us train ourselves to ask ourselves first: What did I do to evoke a response like that? Often we get very great light on ourselves when we do this. I think this is a very humble approach, a very valid approach to sisterly living.

Now let us look at some of the strong thoughts the Church puts before us in her beautiful Latin hymns. *Creator Alme Siderum* speaks of our dear Lord being "urged on by generous love". This is always at the heart of Advent: that we are urged on, that we are hurrying, rising up, casting off darkness. The Church says to our Lord, "urged on by a generous love, you, Lord Jesus, became a healing power for a sick world". I think that is wonderfully meaningful for us in our contemplative vocation. This is what we are called to be, isn't it? Not healing hands exactly, because we do not have an active apostolate, but a healing power for a sick world. God knows that if our world was ever sick, it is certainly sick now. This is our vocation. This is what we are to realize anew in Advent, how to be a healing power. We are not to produce the medicine; we are not to be the healing hands, but a healing power. And to do this we must do it in the way that Christ became a healing power: he was urged by a generous love, a love that desired to give and give and that drove him on. It pushed him on; it pressed him on.

Then in the hymn at Lauds, *Verbum Supernum*, we ask God to "inflame our hearts by the fire of love and empty them of earth's fleeting desires". It is quite a painful process to empty out a heart of earthly desires. The more interior the desire, the more difficult and painful it is to remove it. But the Church tells us in her very realistic way that it is only hearts that are emptied of worldliness, of earth's fleeting desires, that God can inflame with his love. Empty out your hearts; turn them upside down; pour out all these things so that the liquid love of God can flow into them.

We say to our Lord in this First Week of Advent, "Show me your ways; teach me your paths." This doesn't mean to point them out as to a tourist, who might say, "Isn't that lovely?" but to show me your ways that I may walk on them, and teach me your paths that I may follow them. This is the itinerary for Advent. Don't sit at the window and rock and wait for the Redeemer to come. Walk down these ways, and follow these paths. It is a time of action.

A homily of St. Gregory the Great speaks of our Lord's desire to find us prepared. This is a very poignant thought. We know our desire to bring him forth, our desire to meet him in the Parousia, our desire to be with him forever. He has desires, too. He desires our perfection. He desires to find us prepared. He will be very disappointed if we are not prepared. If we meet him at midnight Mass with our little works of darkness still around us as snugly as a shawl, then he will be disappointed, because he is desiring to find us ready; he is desiring to finds those hearts emptied of our pet affections, our worldliness; he is desiring to find us stripped of our works of darkness; he is desiring to find us full of love and gentleness and eagerness to be his. So let us not disappoint him; let us not meet him with hearts full of our own little desires.

In the solemn responsory at Matins of the First Sunday of Advent, the Church says, "Rush out to meet him." The Latin word does not mean "walk out". The Church doesn't say, "Stroll out to meet him." This is our Redeemer, our God. And so if we see him coming, we rush out to meet him. This is what we have to do in these weeks when we see the opportunities he will send. These are all pre-Christmas encounters with him. Let us rush out and throw our arms around them, the way he did around his Cross. Let us be eager for him, eager to grow in his likeness, eager to beget and build his life within us. Let us not saunter along; let us rush out, hurry out to meet him.

I know that each one of us will be turning these beautiful phrases from the liturgy round and round in her prayer. What more can the Church do to help us pray, to help us deepen our union with God this Advent? He is coming, and we should cast off our works of darkness and rush out to meet him, with our hearts empty of everything that gets in the way of his love pouring in. Let us strive to be full of light as we prepare to rush into the arms of grace, toward God, toward every opportunity to love him and to grow in his likeness.

✢ ✢ ✢ ✢

TUESDAY OF THE FIRST WEEK OF ADVENT

Wonder

*I give you praise, Father, Lord of heaven and earth, for although
you have hidden these things from the wise and the learned you
have revealed them to the childlike* (Lk 10:21).

THE HUMAN HEART is always filled with some kind of
wonder. It is one of the first signs of the growing awareness of a small child. Who has not smiled to see a little
infant discovering that he has feet, he has hands! He waves
them about and looks at them. He is full of wonder!
Then, as he grows he becomes more and more full of
wonder at the things he can do. He can move; he can
walk. Wonder is so radical to the human heart. But it is
we who decide what kind of wonder fills our hearts.
Sometimes there can be a depressive wonder: Why does
God permit the things he does? Or, we wonder about
ourselves. We wonder how, after all the graces of Advent,
we can still be so faulty and faltering. But all of these
human wonderings, which, left to themselves, can become a dark wonder, must be changed into the wonder of
light, that God does know exactly what he is about. There
are so many things that we cannot understand in the
world, that we cannot understand in one another, and,
most deeply, that we cannot understand in ourselves. But
in all of these we are full of wonder that God is neverthe-
less working out his own Divine plans.

Let these precious hours of Advent be given to wonder.
When we feel depressed by our faults, let us wonder that
God can forgive us so much; let us be filled with wonder

and praise that God goes on believing in us, hoping in us, and trusting that we will somehow yet realize his dream of us. I love to watch the flower bulbs in the community room putting their little shoots through what looks like a dark tangle of mulch. If these were sentient bulbs, I think they might say, "This is too hard. How can I push through such a tangle of things?" Yet out of this rather depressing-looking tangle come up these tiny, pure white heads. We can learn so much from the bulbs. We are like sentient bulbs and we cannot say, "I cannot push through; it's too hard." We who have grace, who have power given us by God, we *can* push through. And so I think it is a very solid Advent practice to pray, "God, grant me the grace to push through. Grant me the grace to realize my own possibilities, to realize your dream of me."

For God is looking at *us* and giving us the grace to wonder what we can do with his help. We should be filled with wonder at our possibilities, at his hope in us, at his dream of us. We shall take that great faculty of wonder into eternity, so let us never misuse it with thoughts like: "Why do things have to be this way? Why is another person doing these things? Why did it turn out that way?" Dark wonder is a terrible thing, because it is a misuse of a power we shall take into eternity where we shall wonder at the wondrousness of God forever and ever. We shall wonder at our salvation forever and ever.

In eternity many expressions of our humanity will cease; there will be no hunger or thirst—but wonder will be eternally there, the wonder of God. There will be nothing then to say to one another but, "Holy, Holy, Holy." This wonder which perdures for all eternity is, like all wonder, a growing wonder. That is why the chorus of the blessed is not one "Holy", but instead they keep crying out to one another—because the wonder grows. We want to use this great faculty, which will find its fullness in eternity, as God wishes us to use wonder.

In these Advent days, let us wonder more than ever before that God should have chosen such a way as he did to save us. Who could have dreamed that the almighty, omnipotent God would enter into humanity in such a way and in such circumstances? According to our human reckoning it was all wrong. The place was wrong; the situation was wrong. There were no human worshipers at first, and the angels themselves quickly disappeared into the night. Be filled with wonder at God's way of doing things! And then be full of wonder at the way he lived. With all his miraculous powers, with all his infinite love, he was rejected by so many and yet he went on. He was not thanked, but he went on. By some he was not loved, but he went on. We are filled with wonder above all at the pinnacle of redemption, the triumph of his love. Again we would say that this was all wrong, to be reduced to such a condition, tortured and bleeding to death on a cross. But it was the triumph of his love. Let us be filled with wonder at God's way of doing things and apply this to our lives.

We want to be filled with wonder and with praise, as our Lady's heart was filled with wonder and praise. In the cave at Bethlehem she was filled with wonder. And under the Cross she was filled with wonder. This is the great invitation of Advent, that we should not misuse that sense of wonder that God has put into every human heart. Let us never be filled with dark wonder at the things that go wrong and the things that are wrong, but let us be filled with wonder that God can make all things right and that he will, if we allow him. Let us be filled with the greatest wonder that he chose to come in such guise that we could hold him to our hearts, that he came small enough for us to take into our arms. May we be filled with wonder at God's love, at God's forgiveness, at God's unswerving hope in us. Let us never misuse wonder, this faculty that we shall take into eternity.

❖ ❖ ❖ ❖

Right Nutrition

Jesus took the seven loaves and the fish, gave thanks, broke the loaves. . . . All ate and were satisfied (Mt 15:36, 37).

WE ALL KNOW in daily experience in this blessed Advent season that there are such rich viands spread out before us in the liturgy that one hardly knows where to linger. One thinks, "This must be the theme of my prayer today", and then the next responsory comes, and then this reading comes, and then this lesson comes. In a beautiful, provocative homily by Saint Bernard at Matins we read a wonderful phrase: "Feed on goodness." We should, spiritually, watch what we are eating.

Now, each of us has full command over what our thoughts feed upon. There is a great thrust in our times about right nutrition. There is finally a reaction against the eating of junk foods, which not only provide no nourishment but do great harm to the physical system. Reputable doctors are saying that we are what we eat. Sometimes people deliberately feed themselves on wrong foods, junk foods, which taste good at the moment, please the palate at the moment—but give no nourishment for the body's growth and sustenance, and little by little work destructive havoc on the body. We can do this spiritually as well. "Feed on goodness." How can we live a spiritual life, how can we be the force that we are called to be in the Church of God, beginning with the local church of our community, if our diet is very destructive, if, instead of feeding on goodness we feed on self? Do we sometimes feed our thoughts on impatience, feed them on self-pity? Do we feed on irritability? Do we feed on grudging giving? Do we feed on selfishness, instead of feeding on goodness?

Saint Bernard says, "Remember to eat your bread, or your heart will wither." We must remember to eat our bread, to feed on goodness, or our spiritual life will wither. It really will. What are some of those "junk foods" of the spiritual life?

One junk food is certainly—pardon me for the forthright term—the "greasiness" of self-pity. We know that physically the elements of grease are very destructive of the human body. That grease of self-pity eats away at the strength of one's spiritual life. We want to think about that. Doctors are saying, "Don't eat all this grease. This is why the United States leads the world in heart problems." But what do we eat spiritually? What slows down the spiritual heart? What makes it sluggish? What makes it arrhythmic? What gives it bad fibrillations? Certainly, self-pity.

Doctors also warn against an abundance of spices, the insistence that everything has to be spiced up, as they say. Well, is this not impatience in the spiritual life? Impatience and irritability, the junk foods of the spiritual life, provide pleasure by the moment and destroy us by the hour.

Then, there is surely the junk food of sentimentality in the spiritual life: I have sweet thoughts, and I have sweet resolutions—and that's it. I often do not get to anything deeper than that. Sentimentality will certainly not take us very far at all in our spiritual lives. And yet we know we can be tempted to rest in that. We want to "feel" good when we pray. We make easy resolutions which we do not follow through with the strength to keep: living on the upper surface of our own life, without really going down into the depths of it. This is certainly a junk food comparable to too many sweets on the physical level— another thing that they say is destroying the health of our American people. And we can do this in the spiritual life, and then get to the place that, if prayer doesn't taste good, I don't pray. If this really takes effort, and I don't feel myself sweetened, then I don't make the effort. That is another junk food.

Besides sentimentality and self-pity and the impatience of spiciness, there is the desiccated food which is a lack of generosity: "I don't want to get involved. I don't really want to give myself." I don't give my full share in community. Each one's share is everything she can possibly give. If we are not giving that full share, then we are feeding spiritually on a dried-out diet: desiccated foods, which have lost their nutritive value.

Then, the last example is poisoned food. What could that be? We know it could be only one thing: uncharity. We are eating poison if we are fostering unkind thoughts, uncharitable rememberings, playing little records of criticism within us.

We need to look at these things, all these ugly junk foods of the spiritual life, before we can turn our heads and look at the real nutriments. Of course, they are just the opposite of all these things. Instead of sentimentality, there is perseverance in prayer. What does it matter how I feel? It is God I am concerned about, just to be there with him, to respond to him in all kinds of weather. That's all that matters. That is the true food. Instead of the greasiness of self-pity, there is gratitude: to be so grateful that God thought of creating me; that God thought me worth redeeming; that God actually called me to this very rare vocation. Gratitude and self-pity are utterly incompatible. They will not be roommates. They will not abide at the same time in one heart. Then, instead of that desiccated, nutritionless food of holding back, we want total giving, giving everything that is asked of me, and more than is asked of me. There is a wonderful reward for doing everything that is asked of me: I see a lot of things I can do that I wasn't even asked to do. Then, instead of the junk food of impatience and irritability, we must foster sweetness and gentleness: the gentleness which is always one of the great characteristics of strength. Finally, instead of that poisoned food of uncharity, there is love. Love, in season and out of season.

Saint Bernard says, "Feed on goodness and remember to eat your bread." In all of these circumstances, remember to do that. We usually don't forget to come to the refectory! As far as I can see, everybody shows up faithfully three times a day—because we wouldn't be able to live our lives, to do our work, to pray, if we did not have our nourishment. But, we have to be told this spiritually, "Remember to eat your bread, or your heart will wither away." When Saint Bernard says, "Feed on goodness", he is repeating in different words what Saint Paul says: "Everything that is lovely, everything that is admirable, everything that is lofty—let this be the substance of your thoughts." This is what we feed on.

As we move into this week of Advent we need to improve our diet. We need to feed steadily on goodness so that we can be, with God's grace, prepared to meet him at Bethlehem. God is swift to do good. Sometimes we are slow, aren't we? This is no time to be slow! We have to feed on goodness as a steady diet in these weeks, on every occasion looking for this nutritious food of goodness.

Let us help one another in this, because just as a physically well-nourished person shows this—in her complexion, her gait—so do rightly-nourished spiritual persons show this to one another. When someone is continually feeding on goodness, it shows. We need that example. We all see the beauty of right behavior, of charity, of gentleness, of stability in doing good, of fidelity. And this makes us want to look like that, too.

THURSDAY OF THE FIRST WEEK OF ADVENT

The Epicenter

IN TODAY'S Gospel we have our dear Lord's shivering words about the house built on sand, which looked so good, standing there. Everything was going along all right. But then some winds came, and then some rain came. And that good-looking house fell because it was built on sand. Jesus says in those terrible words, which always cause a shiver to go down the spine, "The rains came and the winds came, and that house fell. And, oh, what a fall it had!" We have falls in our lives, in our spiritual lives, and sometimes they are very bad. The trouble is that we had built something on sand.

And then, of course, our dear Lord talks about the other house: it also looked good. It *was* good, because it was built on a rock. He says that the winds came and they beat against that house. If these were sentient houses, we couldn't claim that this house didn't feel the wind, and the other one did. No, it felt the winds. The winds and rain beat upon this house, too. And it also suffered; it also had to endure the impact of the untoward. But this house stood firm because it was built upon a rock.

I remember that when we were beginning the building of the monastery at one of our daughterhouses, the soil-boring studies held up the digging of the foundation for months because of the dangers related to soil subsidence. We were not able to go forward, dig the foundation, put up the building, without really knowing what was under it. While we chafed a bit, wanting them to start at that digging, we did recognize the extreme importance of knowing this. Because of this problem of soil subsidence, we have the foundation of this house measured off into sections. When I made visitation there, I could see this. There were extra-wide seams in the floors; in the naked concrete, you could see it very well. They took precautions in the building. First, they didn't build on sand. And then they took precautions so that if, despite their best efforts, something happened, it wasn't going to wreck the whole place. If part of this soil gave way three-eighths of an inch, the building was not going to tilt, because extra work had been done.

Another image that comes to mind is the recent earthquake in California. At the time we heard a great deal about the epicenter, where the tremor of the earthquake is usually the most violent and the land is most in danger. Each of us needs to ask this Advent, what is my epicenter? What is my greatest danger point? Where do I have to take most precautions? In the earthquake in California, we heard about this fault running through the earth, twelve miles beneath the surface. At times, the weakest point in our spiritual lives is more than twelve miles down!

We want to see what this is. We want, without putting ourselves under a microscope, to take better precautions, so that God's house, which is each of us, does not fall when the rains beat against it or the winds beat against it or the earthquake comes. We need to ask: What caused this? If I lapse into a sodden moodiness or indulge miasmic sensitiveness, is there perhaps a resentment or self-pity I have never resolved twelve miles beneath that epicenter? If I quake with anger over something that even I myself can see, later on, is really such a small thing, what is twelve miles below that epicenter? Where is the real trouble? The real trouble would be that I have not exercised self-control in little things. I have not been faithful to little disciplines that all our customs call for.

In the area of holy poverty, am I shaken with seismic rumblings if I want something and it is not there? I want this, I want that, and I want it right away. Twelve miles below this reaction is the fault of never having penetrated the meaning of my vow to be "without *anything* of my own". That is where the real trouble is. Why am I so upset if somebody seems to usurp *my* little place or *my* little things?

We wonder why people build over the fault, where the danger is greatest. But surely, our dear Lord could say to us: "How can you think you are building on rock when you have never taken care of that fault which is twelve miles down? Why are you so foolish?" Then the comparison ends, because this geological mystery cannot be remedied by man. But we *can* bring the plates together; we *can* mend the fault, that deep-down thing twelve miles below the surface of this occasion, this situation in which I gave such a bad performance, and this is wonderful. I really can bring meaning and practice together, so that the earthquake does not happen again. I do not despond, I do not wed myself to this mood, I do not sit down in self-pity, I do not erupt into anger. I can do what the scientists can't do, what all the geologists in the world can't do. But I have the grace to do it, and I *can* do it.

This is an intriguing subject. I ask you to explore it very deeply in prayer. Let us look, each one of us, at our own epicenter, when something unexpected comes up or when something seems to build up, and there is this wreckage. Then I have to see what is really twelve miles below it. And I have to see this, not in a pessimistic dismay, but in what I would dare to call an affirmative dismay, and say, "Yes, that's horrible! That is frightening; but I *can* do something about it."

❖ ❖ ❖ ❖

A Pattern of Giving

IN THE first reading, Isaiah speaks of those who were "disposed to evil" (Is 29:17-24; *note*: the present translation is "alert to do evil"). This happens to all of us at times: a phrase that we have often heard in the Scriptures leaps out at us with such vehemence that we feel we have never heard this before. I was very shaken by this terrible term, to be "disposed" to do evil. What does this mean? Not just that they did evil, as all of us do on occasion. Anything that offends God, any infidelity, is evil. But they were disposed to this. This is the way they tended. What does it mean to be disposed to good? It does not mean that on occasion we do good, and that on occasion we are joyful, on occasion we are happy, and on occasion we are grateful, but that we tend that way. That's the way we would go unless we did violence to ourselves. All the ways that we use that word "disposed" started swimming around in my heart.

We speak of a person as having a very sweet disposition. We mean that this is her pattern. It is not something for an occasion, but this is what we have come to expect of this person: she has such a lovely disposition, such a good disposition. And we know what we mean, too, when we say, "Oh, my goodness! She just has such a bad disposition", or "This person has such a churlish disposition." This is the pattern; this is the way this person has made us expect her to be. And then we speak of a person being well disposed. We say, "We can ask this person's

49

help because she is well disposed toward the community."
Again we mean that this person tends toward doing good
to us. Or we say another nation is well disposed to our
country, meaning that this nation is our ally, it tends
toward our interest. And we speak of a person, a group, or
a nation as being ill disposed. They tend toward bringing
upon us what is not good, what is ill, what is the opposite
of good.

A tremendous country for exploration opens out before
us in this word, "disposition". One very beautiful meaning
speaks of being totally given to another. This is certainly
the aim of all of us: we want to be totally at God's disposition. He can do whatever he wants with us. He can keep
us well, or he can let us be ill; he can let things go well
(according to our superficial way of looking at things), or
he can let them go in a very suffering way; he can ask us to
do something we think we cannot do or something very
difficult, or he may seem to ask us to do very little; he may
call us to be in the foreground, or he may place us in the
background.

Saint Thérèse of Lisieux used a charming little figure of
a ball that could be bounced. She wanted to be so much at
God's disposal that he could literally bounce her around in
whatever place he wanted, whatever situation he wanted,
whatever circumstance he wanted, with whatever personal feelings he would allow to be in her. This is a very
wonderful aim: to want to be bounced, to be able to be
bounced around by God, and, yes, to be bounced around
in community. I am the one they call on to do anything
at all. I am totally at the community's disposition. I am
"on call".

To be disposed toward good means that we *are* doing it.
We are more and more disposed toward doing good when

we do it more and more. Our Lady was disposed toward holiness. The privilege of her Immaculate Conception gave her a disposition toward good that we do not have. Being pre-redeemed she did not come into this world with the burden of original sin and the downward pull of concupiscence. Still, she did, all her life, dispose herself toward good. She was a real human being—an immaculate one, yes, but with the same possibilities of choice. We feel a kind of shudder of awe as we speak this great truth. Our Lady, free from original sin, but still a human being who had choices to make and therefore could have done wrong, would have been far more culpable than any of us if she had chosen to sin. Her Immaculate Conception did not mean that she was incapable of wrongdoing in her choices. She was preserved from an inheritance of sin, but she still had her own life choices to make.

The first choice we know about is at the Annunciation, which shows us very clearly her disposition toward humility in the way she responded. She thought of herself as a handmaid, and so at this most startling revelation ever made by God to man, she responded with that same humility toward which she was disposed. Even though she was deeply troubled, as the Scriptures tell us, and obviously afraid, her disposition was toward whatever God asked. She responded, "Behold the handmaid of the Lord", because this was her disposition, to be a little servant. The handmaid was the lowest of the low among the servants. Our Lady was disposed toward being the lowliest of all, and because of that, she could carry over this disposition into being the Mother of God, the greatest human being who ever lived or ever will live, the most singular, the most loved by God, the only immaculate human being. She kept her disposition of handmaidenship.

We see this all through her life. She is the little hand-maid who goes off to Bethlehem without a house for him to be born in; she is the little handmaid who flees into Egypt when, through his messenger in the middle of the night, God says, "Go to this strange land where you know nobody." She is the little unquestioning handmaid when he says, "Why did you seek me?" She did not understand, yet did not demand a detailed explanation. She returned home to Nazareth and went about her wifely, motherly, domestic business. She was the little handmaid who stood at the edge of the crowd when our Lord spoke to the multitudes. She did not go up and seat herself beside him as we might think a mother would have a right to do. But her handmaidenship was her disposition and it impregnated, inflamed, everything that she did. On Calvary she stood there weeping: "*Stabat Mater dolorosa, lacrimosa*", but without a word of protest, without an assertion of right. She was the little handmaid to the end. Always that disposition toward good was growing in her, so that what was perfected on Calvary was what had been already present before the Annunciation, at the Annunciation, at Bethlehem, in Egypt, in the temple, at the edge of the crowd, on the way of the Cross—speaking not a word, just being there. Her pattern of goodness was growing by repeated good.

When the Scriptures speak of people disposed to do evil, it means that they were doing it again and again, so that every time a new choice came, their pattern of evil disposed them even less toward making a good choice. We can turn that around and think of being disposed toward good from doing it over and over again. Every time we choose how to deal with our impatience, we are more disposed to be patient the next time our patience is tried. Every time we step forward in the service we were not expecting to be asked for, that we do not feel like doing, we are more disposed to be generous, to be given, to be self-forgetful. On the contrary, every time we say a sharp word, a harsh word, an angry word, we are more disposed to say it a little louder and a little faster in the next situation like that. But, each time that we put down that inner turbulence and respond in a loving, sweet, soothing, and smoothing way, we are more disposed toward good the next time, and it becomes less and less difficult. This is wonderful.

It is a very large acreage of reflection that opens out, and an awesome one, too, in the thought that we are charting our own dispositions every day. By the way we dispose ourselves to tend this Advent, we dispose ourselves to tend at Christmastide. Let us pray for one another, that we may be disposed toward good. We shall sometimes fall; we shall sometimes make mistakes. But when we are daily deepening and strengthening that pattern of being disposed toward good, we will see more quickly what was wrong and be more quickly energized to make right what was wrong.

The memory comes into my mind of a toy I had as a child. This kind of toy was fashioned in the shape of a little rubber animal, or sometimes it was a little figure. You could push it over, but it always came back and stood upright. This fascinated me. I would push and I would push to be sure it was going to come back each time. I remember doing that over and over and thinking, "Will it be able to do that the next time?" And it always came back. Because of the way the rubber toy was made, its disposition was always to stand up, so that when it fell it was disposed to stand up again.

We have the grace, we have the choice, and we decide whether we shall be disposed to fall, disposed to do wrong, or disposed to do good. Let us make this a deep, deep Advent theme that we are, in our Lord's sight, like that poor little toy; we will fall, and sometimes things will seem to bowl us over. But we will come back because we are disposed to good. This is what we want to do; this is the pattern that we want to strengthen, a pattern of giving.

❖ ❖ ❖ ❖

SATURDAY OF THE FIRST WEEK OF ADVENT

Knowing the Need to Be Forgiven

Little Chapter at First Vespers of Sunday

DEAREST SISTERS, Advent is the season in which we are constantly saying to God: "Come." We are issuing an invitation, almost a command, so lovingly imperious is the liturgy: "Come." Sometimes we dare to say to him, "Come quickly." We know that this prayer can be made only by one who is herself coming. It is not as though we stand still and call out our imperious command to God that he should come. When we really say, "Come", we are, almost without thinking about it, reaching out our arms and stepping forward. And so, coming always concerns a moving of two persons.

We want to be "go-ers" in this great season of "come". We want to be going each day toward Bethlehem, toward the mystery of a humble God, a poor God, a little God. In the Advent liturgy, we find a wealth of tenderness; we are immersed in love and in beauty. We find also much mystery. We find that we must ponder very deeply and beg the Holy Spirit to help us understand what is being said to us in the teaching of our Mother the Church, which is her liturgy.

We find this astonishing mystery in the little chapter of today's Vespers, when Saint Paul in writing to his Thessalonians says some astonishing things. What is he praying for them? He says, one might say, almost coolly, "May the God of peace make you perfect in holiness." Then he goes on to say that his prayer is that God should find his disciples (in which company, of course, Saint Paul always places himself) irreproachable when he comes. What can this mean, dear sisters? How can the Church put this upon our own lips, that we should be perfect in holiness and irreproachable when God comes? How does one, the Apostle himself included, put this together with other sayings of his when he loudly, vigorously describes himself as the first of sinners? "He came to save sinners, of whom I am the greatest", he says.

We want to spend Advent, with the aid of the Holy Spirit, plumbing this mystery more and more. This is the inspired Word of God, and so it is something from which we cannot escape. We are supposed to be made perfect in holiness, and we are to be found irreproachable at the coming of God. Who of us would ever say, "I am without reproach"? We know, always, that we are so worthy of reproach. And in our more lucid moments, in our deepest prayer, we know that if we had offended God only once in all of our lives, we would be worthy of all reproach.

Now, the word *irreproachable*, we know, means "blameless". Must it not then become evident that to be blameless is to be without blame for anyone except ourselves? This is indeed to be blameless, that God finds in us no blaming of others, no reproaching of others. This is one facet of being irreproachable. It means that all our reproach is reserved for ourselves, that we are not usurping the place of God as the judge, the reproacher, the lawgiver, the great decider, the one who separates the sheep from the goats, and his own from those who are not his own. So, we do not usurp his place. We reproach only ourselves.

Then, there is a second facet of this great, mysterious

truth: that our sin, our faultiness, can be, and will be, completely exonerated and erased by God if we live in the truth, by acknowledging our total blameworthiness. Often we have reflected that the words of Scripture are sometimes too familiar to us, that is, we have heard them too often. Oh, yes, we can recite that passage by heart. We know it so well that perhaps we have never really listened to it on its deepest level.

In the liturgy, the great poet of the Advent, Isaiah, speaks to us with the words that God put on his lips when he says, "Though your sins be like scarlet, they may become white as snow. Though they be crimson red, they may become white as wool" (Is 1:18). God will do this for us when we live in the truth, when we come humbly to beg pardon in acknowledging the truth about ourselves.

This begins with our faults. It doesn't begin with our scarlet sins, although truly a consecrated person should feel everything scarlet with sin that is offensive to God. But when we come knowing that we have nothing to plead for us except our misery, acknowledged in the face of God's mercy, we shall receive the fulfillment of this remarkable, almost incredible, Word of God through his prophet that, yes, he can make us irreproachable: white as snow, white as wool. Not if we pretend that it is not so scarlet, not so crimson, or maybe it is someone else's fault, or maybe it is situational, or maybe it is circumstantial. If we come full of excuses we, so to speak (if I may dare use such a phrase), paralyze God.

Surely this is what is meant when the Apostle says he wants God to find us irreproachable at his coming—that we are not reproaching anyone else, or anything else; but that we are humble, without excuse, blameless in the sense of not blaming anyone except ourselves. Then, and then only, can God make us irreproachable and perfect in holiness.

What does that word *perfect* basically mean? A thing, an object, a person, a principle that is perfect is one in which all the parts are exactly what they should be. This is the radical meaning of the word. When is a human being perfect? When everything is in order and all the parts are together the way they should be—which, for a creature of God, means that this creature is utterly humble before him. This is the great God, and I am so small before him, humbled to the dust, knowing that I am worthy of all blame and reproach, that I do not deserve anything from God. I did not even deserve to be created, much less to be redeemed. This is basically, philosophically, metaphysically what it is for a human being to be perfect—that is, for a fallen human being. Our Lady's perfection was different. Our Lord's perfection in his divine humanity was different. But for every fallen creature, our perfection is when all things are in their proper order. And they are in their proper order—let me repeat it—when I know that I deserve nothing: I deserve no mercy; I deserve no more chances; I deserve no more forgiveness. Then all is in order.

Does this not explain how Saint Paul can say he wants us to be perfect in holiness and irreproachable? He also says, "Christ Jesus came into the world to save sinners. Of these I myself am the worst" (1 Tim 1:15). It seems so very clear that this is what he means; he can't mean anything else. This is why, when great Paul says the one and the other, he is saying exactly the same thing in different phrasing.

We want to live this Advent as never before. God is coming to redeem me, and, oh, how I need to be redeemed! How little I deserve to be redeemed again and again! This is the truth that sets us free. The truth makes us, not despondent, never discouraged or depressed, but happy—happy to be without any claim on God except our need, our great crying need of God's love and mercy.

What is it to be true? It is to be without pretense. It is to be without excuse. It is to be without justification, because the meting out of justice pertains to God alone, as he has said so very clearly. (If I may dare to use the verb: God, so to say, "resents" it very much when we try to mete out justice for him.) These are the three properties of truth.

Even in material things, such as a work of art or a work of science, we say, "It's really true", when there is no pretense about it. This art form is valid, this gathering together of scientific effort and production is true, when there is no pretension. We know that the "untrue" artists used to correct their statuary by filling in defects with wax and making it look like that was part of the granite, part of the stone. This was false; it was not true. It was a pretense. We want to look at whether we are putting wax in the cracks of ourselves. The worst place of all that we can ever put it is in our estimate of ourselves. For it is our true self, with all the cracks, all the crevices, all the nicks and the knocks and the discolorations, that at least is true. And God can always work with what is true. God can always save what is true. To be without pretense is to be true.

To be without excuse and to be without justification— this also is to be true. It is this truth which our dear Lord promised would make us free. Allowing God to be my truth means that I allow him to be my excuse, my justification. We should love to pray very simply to God, especially in Advent. He knew all my sins, all my faults, in advance, and certainly I shall never deceive him about them. In his sight I can never blame them on anyone else or on any circumstance. But, this accepted, he himself is my excuse, my justification. That is what I mean by my simple prayer: "God, you knew all these things in advance, and you still made me, and you still are coming to renew the mystery of the redemption, which was for me. You knew these things when you called me here. You knew them when you called me to vows." God loves to be allowed to be our excuse and our justification. We have no other.

Following upon this, I think that to be true is to have become incapable of thinking that we can achieve holiness on our own. To be made "perfect in holiness" does not mean to grow "perfect", to "advance in perfection", as those terms are sometimes used (not very correctly), but to know that we cannot achieve this on our own. It is only by abandoning ourselves to God in the truth, the humbling and so ennobling truth about ourselves, that we can achieve holiness through him and know that we are incapable of achieving it on our own.

To be true also is to be forgiven: to know how much we need forgiveness and to bow our proud heads and accept and receive forgiveness as a great gift. Perhaps those who think they have no need to be forgiven are in the sorriest state that anyone could ever be in. To be true is to know my need and my poverty. It is to know my unworthiness and to know my willfulness, to know my errancy. And this is to be in a state when God can make us holy.

So, dearest sisters, in all the tenderness of Advent, this is very important. The sweetness of Advent is wedded to that great mystery of Advent which begins with the call: Now is the time. Now is the hour. Wake up and be made perfect in holiness, so that at Christmas God will find you irreproachable. We know that if a human being was prostrate on the ground before another, and with many tears was acknowledging all her faults and all her shortcomings and everything she had done to cause hurt, no normal person with a spark of love would keep heaping abuse or blame upon her. We know that, with all our weakness and all our failures, what we want to do is reach out and lift the person up. We would want to embrace the person. That is the image of God in us. And so it is that when *we* are prostrate in the dust (from which we came) before him, so humbled, so needy, confronting the truth, this is when *he* lifts us up and makes us irreproachable by saying: "Yes, those sins, they are scarlet. Yes, those sins, they are crimson red. And I will make them white! White as snow, white as wool."

I offer you these thoughts which have so inflamed my heart during this Advent that we may understand better what it is to be made perfect in holiness, and what it is that prevents us from being holy, prevents all the parts from being where they should be: humbled, prostrate before God, knowing the need of mercy and forgiveness, so aware of one's own faults. I ask that we ponder and pursue this mystery, and that we take these great words of the Advent liturgy very, very seriously. Only thus can we really have the joy of Advent. And this is what God wishes to give us.

SECOND WEEK OF ADVENT

✢ ✢ ✢ ✢

Giving Evidence

THE CHURCH is saying to us again and again, "Now is the acceptable time" (2 Cor 6:2). This Advent will never come again. Perhaps God will bless us with other Advents, although, with the condition the world is in right now, one could have large question marks about that. But even if he does, this one will never come again. We recall the classic words of the poet: "The tender grace of a day that is gone will never come back to me." The graces of this day will never come again. The opportunities for being loving and humble and generous and self-forgetful in this day will never come again. That is a large thought, and we should fill our minds with large thoughts in this season.

In the liturgy of this Sunday, the Church is saying, "You have to do something." And she is saying, "I want to see something." As I was reflecting in prayer on these three readings which our wise Mother the Church puts before us, our dear Lord showed me that, in a sense, we need to "read" them backward—that the conclusion, the very strong point, is in the Gospel: we begin there and then go back and see how these fruits appear.

We have in the Gospel of Saint Matthew the narrative of Saint John the Baptist. This may seem somewhat in disaccord with the tenderness of the season, whereas it is actually in complete accord. His first word on this great Advent mission to announce and then to reveal the coming of Christ, linking the whole Old Testament to the New, is, "Repent!" (Mt 3:2). It is an Advent word. He goes on to say very sternly to the Pharisees and to us, "Produce good fruit as evidence of your repentance." For if we are really doing this, there will be evidence. We cannot be working in all earnestness, with God's grace, to overcome our faults, our blatant faults and our hidden faults, without evidence being given. The community will see it. We will see it if a sister is working very hard not to be involved with herself but to be involved with the things of God and with the community, with the things of the Church. The evidence will be there. If a sister is concerned about working with what she knows in herself are tendencies to a lack of generosity, to selfishness, the evidence will be there; we will see it. If a sister is deepening her prayer life, the evidence will be there.

The second reading, from Romans, tells us what evidence God expects to appear: "May the God of endurance and encouragement grant you to think in harmony with one another" (Rom 15:5). The former translation expressed it as: "live in harmony". How do we live in harmony? Well, we know that, in the world of music, from which the figure is taken, we have to be concerned with the other voices. If it's "Me, me, me—I am a soprano, and I sing my part", and I have no thought about blending with the altos or the tenors or the second sopranos, and I keep my own time and make my own interpretation, then, even if I have a lovely, lyric voice, I am a disaster for the choir. The Epistle is presenting this concern for others in community living, living in harmony. I cannot be self-focused.

God is calling us to live in harmony, which is always a going out. I believe I have mentioned in times past a facet of harmony: that when you are singing in harmony, you don't sing by ear—you sing the score. Somebody may have an ear for harmony, and so she doesn't sing the notes that are written but instead sings something that "harmonizes"—except it doesn't belong with the organ accompaniment, and it doesn't fit at all with what the third voice is singing. And so it is destructive because it is a "me" thing: this is my own harmonic line here that I invent; it is not in the score. And so it is with living in community: it has to be in the score. We follow our observance, we follow recommendations, and we follow the score, which is written by God. We do not, as it were, "sing it by ear", because then we distort the score, we distort the accompaniment, and we make it impossible for the other voices to sing.

This is what I mean by "reading back". If we are giving evidence of really repenting and looking at our dear Lord and not at ourselves, of looking at the needs of the Church and not at ourselves, then we will be a sign of encouragement to one another and not a discouragement. This encouragement that we give to one another in God-focused living, in real concern not for myself but for others, is a reaching out to all the hardships and miseries of the world. How many persons throughout the world have nothing of what we have—do not have the care, do not have the food, do not have shelter. Millions of people are so suffering, so alone, so untended. If our life is reaching out, we do encourage them; the evidence shows.

We "read back" to the first reading, where Isaiah says that it is not by appearance that God judges, nor is it by hearsay that he decides (Is 11:3). Now, this has something to do with harmony and evidence. We want to ask ourselves some searching questions: Do I go by hearsay? This is the way something affects me, something offends me, something hurts me, and immediately I react against it.

Often it's hearsay, it is not the truth at all, it is never what was meant; it is just that I am so involved in myself that I am ready, on the basis of this hearsay, to misjudge; I lapse into self-pity; I become more self-involved. Then, of course, I disturb the harmony to which we are called in the Sunday liturgy, and I am not giving the evidence that the Church calls me to account for, this Sunday.

I cannot read this in a detached way and say that Saint John the Baptist is talking only to those Pharisees. We each must look into ourselves. This is the beginning of repentance. I place myself in that crowd where the Church places me on Sunday. This is one of the wonderful things that has been emphasized so much by Vatican Council II: that God is present in his living Word when it is read, and that when the Word of God is proclaimed in the liturgy, he is speaking directly to each one of us. And so, in the Sunday Gospel when the Word of God says to you and to me, "Produce good fruit as evidence of your repentance", I have to respond. The Church is calling me to account, through the mouth of her prophet. Let it be a week of evidence.

✤　✤　✤　✤

God's Mercy and Love

MY DEAR SISTERS, throughout Advent we say again and again, "Lord, show us your mercy and love." And so I thought I must speak about mercy. We are so familiar with that word "mercy", that perhaps we have not really plumbed its depths as we should. The Latin word *misericordia* is profound and perhaps more readily puts before us the real meaning of *mercy*. It is the heart, the *cor*, that is full of pity for the misery of others. We should love to linger in prayer on what it means to have a heart, literally, for the miserable, for the poor. Who are the poor? We are the first of them. Sometimes we do not try to fathom the depths of the fact that no one is happy with her faults. Perhaps it is when we are most energetic about trying to excuse them or pass them over or pretend that it is somebody else's fault that we are the most miserable. Who of us would stand up and say, "Well, there is nothing wretched about me. I don't need any pity. I have no afflictions. There is nothing distressing in me." No, in our lucid moments (and I'm sure this is one of them), we know we need mercy very much. We need the mercy of God, who is moved by our misery.

We see this again and again in the New Testament. Jesus' Heart was moved with pity for the miseries of others and not only for their illnesses, for their bereavement, but even in their ordinary human needs. His Heart was moved with pity for the crowd who had nothing to eat. He did not say they could get something later; there was a need right then, and his Heart reached out. This is what God does.

Mercy makes God refrain from punishing. Mercy is kindness that is in excess of what fairness could demand. It is most of all something enduring. It is a disposition to forgive. Mercy is not a situational thing. It is a disposition, something abiding; and this disposition to reach out in forgiveness makes us resemble God, the great Forgiver, the great Pardoner, the untiring mercy-Giver.

Another definition for *misericordia* is "tenderhearted-ness", which means that we not only look with sorrow on the faults and needs and miseries of others but we suffer with them, in *compassion*. That is a beautiful, beautiful word: "to suffer with". We are told again and again in the New Testament that this is why our dear Lord took on our lowly humanity. As God, from all eternity, he could and he did have pity on us, but he could not suffer our human sufferings without taking on our humanity. And so he did, in order to be the compassionate One who knew what it was to have our ordinary needs—to be hungry, to be cold, to know the hurt of not being thanked, to suffer the deep pain of seeing how his teaching seemed not to penetrate, how all his loving exhortative words (for instance, about humility) seemed quite lost upon his apostles. Always his human compassion—not just his Deific pardon—went on and on, far beyond their bickering and their petty ambitions.

At Matins there was such a marvelous line in Isaiah (he's full of marvelous lines). It just charmed me, and made me smile broadly to myself. It said, "They turned to the Lord in their misery and he was won over" (Is 19:22). What a delightful phrase! It is wonderful that God revealed this already in the Old Testament. I think we could dare to translate it that he can be cajoled; he can be persuaded into giving us another chance. We can win him over just by being so sorry and showing him our misery. We, poor sinners, come crawling to him in our misery. We've committed the same fault again. We all set out in Advent, "Surely, I will never sin again; never, never, never. I will never commit a fault again. I will never let grace escape unheeded again." And then we fall and come back. Nobody says, "I went to confession five years ago", but "I went last week, and I'll need to go next week." And we could think, "Well, I could easily go every day." This would be a good thing. And I do—in my prayer, in the Confiteor in the evening, in the prayers at Mass.

Far from making us depressed when we see how miserable we are, it is really a step forward that we know it more and more. The more we know it, the less proud we will be when we see what miserable little persons we are, how many graces we have not used, how many occasions there are to which we have not risen, how many times we have given a very poor example. Our miseries really do make us miserable. And may it never be that our miseries do not make us miserable. We pray so often, "His mercy endures forever." Then we want to stop and say, "How long does ours last?" His mercy endures forever. Forever is quite a long time.

We cry out during Advent in a perfectly charming oration (as though he doesn't know it), "Father, we need your help." I know you love this just as I do. We are getting into trouble again and again with our faults and often enough trying to excuse them, but how this prayer reaches his merciful Heart when the Church in these wonderful Offices has us speak like little children: "We need help." We need each other's help, also. We ask him to free us from sin and bring us to life. And when, by our love and our mercy, we free our sisters (in a very deep sense) from their misery, we too are life-bringers. So, we want to call out mercy to one another; we all know we need it very much.

❖　❖　❖　❖

Silence before the Lord God

John went throughout the whole region of the Jordan, proclaiming
a baptism of repentance for the forgiveness of sins (Lk 3:3).

DEAR SISTERS, we want to reflect on the theme of this
Advent Sunday, which is repentance: to realize that our
greatness is to be found only in humility before God. Just
before we began the Advent season, in the Office of
Matins the Church was gathering together her chorus of
minor prophets, each to speak his word for the coming of
the King. We had in Zephaniah a word that seems to me
to be the trumpet call for Advent: "Silence in the house of
the Lord God, for the day of the Lord is at hand" (Zeph
1:7).

There is a silence in Advent that is a silence of waiting.
We say it is a time of silence, of recollection, of deep
interior prayer, a time for the cultivation of passivity before the Lord, as we strive to acquiesce to everything that
he asks. Indeed it is. But the most profound passivity
before God is that most teeming with activity. We agree
to wait upon the Lord, and we agree to do something in
this period of waiting. We are watching for every occasion of his coming. He says to us through the heartbreak-
ing words of Isaiah, "Israel has not known me, my people
has not understood" (Is 1:3). During this Advent he will
be coming to us every day; he is coming to us today with
certain inspirations that will be unique for each one of us.
He will speak in our hearts showing an occasion to give

ourselves, and so our waiting and our watching has to be very alert, very vigilant so that he never has to say to us, "My beloved has not known me and my spouse has not understood." And yet we know how often we must say that this is the truth. We have not been deep enough to get below the surface of things. We see only something that tries us, some circumstance that is not agreeable to us, some misunderstanding that we want to nurse quietly along. And all the time he is in that circumstance, that person, that inspiration to his beloved, and we have not known him and we have not understood. We have lived on the surface of our own lives instead of plunging into the depths.

The prophet Micah says of God in wonder, "You will cast all our sins into the depths of the sea" (Mic 7:19). The magnificence, the munificence of it! But then the horror of it, that we fish them up again! Part of our Advent waiting, a great part of our preparation, our education in what it means to be the little humble ones of the Lord, is that we consent to be forgiven. It is wonderful to forgive, and to show mercy is a great and glorious thing, and it is to act in a Godlike way. If God stopped dispensing mercy for one second we would simply cease to be. We would be annihilated before him. It is only his infinite mercy and his unending compassion that sustain us in being. But there is this very dark streak in the beauty of our creation which makes it sometimes not *want* to receive mercy, not want to be blessedly small enough to hold out our hands for the mercy of God and the mercy of our sisters, to hold up the cup of our hearts for this mercy. Sometimes one of the greatest difficulties of our pride is that we do not wish to consent to be forgiven, to go gratefully through life because God has truly forgiven our sins.

This Advent I would invite you to make this consent to be forgiven because this is a very unique gift to God. He, as God, can show mercy; he cannot receive it. As God, he is the Lord of forgiveness, but he cannot be forgiven. We can say, in our human way of expressing a real truth of God before which all our human language limps and falters, that we can contribute something to God, who cannot be forgiven. And so, let us bring to him in everything that we strive to do this Advent this consent to be forgiven, this gift of being forgiven. When he, with lordly mercy, promises to throw all our faults and our sins into the sea, let us not put on the diving equipment of pride and go right down and bring them up again.

There is something in all of us that would like to pretend that we do not need to be forgiven, and this is why we sometimes get so excited about our faults, why we cannot be simple, why we will not stop rocking that little spiritual monster child that we cuddle so, that we do not want snatched from us, that we do not want laid to Christian burial. We want to keep looking at it and in the end we convince ourselves that it is beautiful. Or, the other alternative is to say that this isn't my child; it is somebody else's. We are adept at choosing one of those two alternatives which save us from being forgiven. So I ask you again, consent to be forgiven and go on to the next grace, the next inspiration so that our Lord doesn't have to say, "I spoke and my beloved didn't understand. I came and she did not know me because she was busy with her faults, polishing them up into pseudo-, quasi-virtues."

This is the greatest insult to God because it is an offense against the truth. Let this be our consolation, that God is truth, and all truth honors him; therefore, the honest admission of our faults gives glory to God. And so, there is no reason to be discouraged because no matter how many faults the light of the coming King brings into focus in our hearts, everything honestly faced can give honor to him. Now isn't that wonderful? Isn't that something to be happy about? Isn't that why we continually rejoice in this season of penance? We laugh together and we are happy together, because this is the whole meaning of Advent, that we are the forgiven ones.

✣ ✣ ✣ ✣

A Cleaned Heart

MY DEAR SISTERS, in the second week of Advent we have
so rich a liturgy encompassing the great solemnity of the
Immaculate Conception of the Blessed Virgin Mary and
rounding its weekly cycle off with the tender feast of Our
Lady of Guadalupe. It is enough to make one feel drunk
with new wine just to think about all that is opening out
before us in this week. We want to linger especially today
on that great solemnity of our Immaculate Mother. It
could be that this great solemnity which is meant to bring
us so close to our Mother could really separate us from her
if we did not enter profoundly into its meaning. She was
immaculate; she was born without sin, and she lived without sin; and death could not hold her in the tomb because
she was without sin and therefore the penalty of death had
nothing to do with her. And so, we could think, what
does this have to do with me? I, who have a whole life of
accumulation of sin and dreary faults committed again and
again. What do we mean—in that prayer of the Church—
that we should come with clean hearts to God? How can
we ever come with a clean heart to God? Is this not
something reserved to our Immaculate Mother? We just
seem to get dirtier and dirtier all the time. How can this
be a real prayer, a sincere prayer? It seems that no sooner
have we got a little bit clean than we are soiled again; and
Scripture itself could seem very depressing when it says
the just man, the man in perfect holiness, falls seven times

a day. We could sit back and say, "Oh, dear!" —and then we want to pray to come to God with a clean heart? None of us would stand up and say, "Well, I am the just woman." But even then I would fall seven times a day!

Is not a *cleaned* heart what Holy Church would have to mean for us poor little ones by a clean heart? We look into this, as I have been looking into it in my own prayer these last days, asking, what do we mean by a clean house? What do we mean by a clean kitchen? There can be something that looks like cleanness just because nothing is going on. Let us linger for a couple of minutes on those material aspects. There are two ways, for instance, you could have a clean kitchen.

One, is that the cook never does anything there, that no service goes on there. Everything is in its proper place and is never taken out; there is no work, there is no love, there is no energy, there is no spending. Nothing is ever spilled because nothing is ever done. Nothing ever burns because nothing is ever cooked. And it's a clean kitchen.

Then, there is the clean kitchen that is the result of loving labor after there have perhaps been some spills, some scorching, some pans boiling over—and then there is always cleaning up. Lots of work has gone on, and wherever human work goes on, there are always going to be some spills, there are always going to be some pans boiling over, and there are always going to be some things that don't turn out as we had hoped. But then it is all cleaned up afterward. That is a very different kind of a clean kitchen from the first kind.

Then too, there is a clean house, the kind of thing we have heard about, read about, shivered about: women who are so tyrannical that they have a spotless house because nobody is ever really allowed to live there. Nothing really happens, in a deeply human sense. It's clean, all right, but for lack of life. And then again, there is a clean house in which a mother of many children has spent herself, every day, cleaning up the mud, sweeping the rug, washing the dishes because people have been fed. You could have very clean dishes if you never fed anyone. You could have a shining stove if nothing is ever cooked on it—going back to our first image. But there can be the house that is always so beautifully clean because the mother is always cleaning up the inevitable messes that human living entails: the happy little disorders that come of living, and the messes that perhaps should not have been made but then should not be pointed at—just cleaned up. And that is a very different kind of clean house.

In our spiritual life, the parallel is very evident: nothing else could be meant by a clean heart but a *cleaned* heart. If the just man falls seven times a day, then he can have a clean heart only by having asked forgiveness seven times, made seven firm purposes of amendment, seven acts of reparation for his faults, seven determinations to go forward. Then he has a cleaned heart.

Our Lady was pre-redeemed. Remember that this means—and one says it with all possible filial reverence—that our Lady was "pre-cleaned". And even that pre-cleaning did not leave her without choices. One grows a little hesitant in the field of her perfect humanity, and awe and reverence are good, but it should not be the wrong hesitation because we should not allow our Lady to become remote from us. The fact that she was free of all human concupiscence, free of all the effects of original sin, does not mean that she was without choices. It does not mean that she could not have chosen to feel sorry for herself. I say, one feels a hesitancy in saying these things, but one shouldn't, because if she never had choices to make in her sinless person, of what purpose would that be? If she were merely some beautiful automaton, she would not be our Mother.

She did not have that downward pull that we have, but she still had choices, and she could have wrong ones or right ones. She could have insisted after the finding in the temple that Jesus explain what he meant. She could have said, "I am your Mother, and I have got to get this straight. I don't understand what you are talking about." But she preferred, she chose, to accept what was to her not understandable, and to return to her humble home and to go about her duties and to ponder these things in her heart. She made her own choice to allow him to fulfill all that was involved in his Passion. And she did not, when she met him on the way of the Cross, lapse into hysterical sobbing, nor did she demand that this should be stopped. She chose the will of God and she chose it freely—again, we say, unencumbered by the downward pull of concupiscence that we know so well, but still a woman quite capable of doing right or wrong, or doing good or better or best.

It is very important that we do not allow our Lady to be distanced from us by her Immaculate Conception, but to be brought closer to us. She is the one to teach us poor sinners because she is called the Refuge of Sinners. Our Lord did not give her to Saint John and say, "Now I am giving her to you, and she is the Mother of all the flawlessly holy ones." But he gave her to be the Mother of all persons, of all men, and he knew what was in man, what is in each one of us, our weaknesses as well as our strengths.

This feast should make us feel very close to her, as we ask her to help us understand what it means to have a cleaned heart. This is at the very heart of our own Franciscan charism: the spirit of conversion, that we are always asking to be forgiven, not in a craven way but in a determined way, always wanting to be cleaned. It is a joyful thing to come humbly before God and say, "I want to come with a clean heart because I have been so often cleaned by you." Every time we confess our faults, every time that we face the truth without the depression born of pride, we are cleaned, and we can come with a clean heart to him. For us to come with a clean heart to God, as the Church asks us to pray, means that I come as one cleansed. And if I have had to be cleansed several million times, that can be transliterated very accurately as saying I have been loved by God several million times, because he has never said, "I've had enough. I cleaned you the last time." But every time he wants to clean us so that we can come to him with a clean heart.

And so, if God shows us our faults or they are lovingly pointed out to us, and we think we are being rubbed very hard and are feeling sorry for ourselves, it is only because God is so intent on cleaning us, so intent on cleansing us: this is a big spot, it needs some hard rubbing; this is a bad stain, it needs a bigger dose of bleach. We grow in the love of being cleansed and in the ongoing understanding of what it means—the only thing it can mean for any of us—to come to God with a clean heart. It means that I have been cleaned by God, by humbly facing the truth, confessing my faults, and wishing to go forward.

✣ ✣ ✣ ✣

Golden Rocks

TODAY I want to talk about rocks. In the beautiful story of Our Lady of Guadalupe entrusted to us by Juan Diego, our Lady came and stood on the rocks. We know that she appeared on barren Tepeyac in winter; there was no verdure around, there was only a heap of rocks. We would think, in our limited way, that this was a rather peculiar place on which she should appear. We hear that in her other apparitions she would appear on a high mountain, she would appear on a cloud, she would appear in a bowered setting. But on Tepeyac she appeared on the rocks, and she did something to the rocks. Do you not remember how Juan Diego told us that she stood on the rocks and they turned to gold? She did not take away the rocks. The rocks did not disappear with her coming; they remained, but became golden.

All of us know that we have rocks in our spiritual lives, and that sometimes we try to "excuse" the rocks and pretend that they are verdant, when they are not. Sometimes we even cling to these rocks and turn from the beauty of self-giving, of humility, to remain on our rocky self-absorption, on our rocks of excuses, our rocks of blaming others—whatever. And we do not allow our Lady to come, not to take them away, but to turn them to gold.

I would like to reflect with you on three particular kinds of rocks. There are black, sooty, muddied rocks, and a rock all muddied up is indeed an ugly thing. Now, to what could one compare this in our spiritual lives, if not to discouragement? It is such a black, dark thing. It is such a muddy thing. What our Lady will do, if we allow her to come and stand on that rock, is to turn it to gold by drawing from it something that is good. In discouragement, which is a very hazardous thing in our life of faith, there is a golden vein underneath: we would really like to be better! When we are so discouraged with ourselves, it is, of course, a mark of pride: we do not wish to see that we are not succeeding, and so we think, "What's the use?" and muddy the situation over.

But it is a wonderful thing that we are not happy with ourselves, because the most terrible thing would be that we are at peace with our faults, absorbed in ourselves, blaming our faults on other people. The fact of discouragement, although very wrong in itself, has a hidden vein of gold. We are sorry it is this way, and we would like it to be different. If we invite our Lady to enter intimately into our spiritual lives and point out to her these black, muddied rocks of discouragement, will she not turn them to gold? We think: What have I done with Advent? Oh, the mistakes I have made—the same old faults, the same old failings. But when we invite her to come upon these rocks of discouragement, that vein of gold can break through and transform the rock. Instead of the mud of discouragement, there is the determination that we will forsake these things, that we will do better because the grace is there. I don't need to blame my faults on other people, on situations. I need to blame them upon myself. I need to look at them and say where the true blame lies. And this already is black turning to gold.

Then there is a second kind of rock, one that is moldy.

I suppose we have all had occasion to see rocks that from dampness have gathered a mold upon them. They are most unbeautiful. And to what could we compare this in our spiritual lives? To that wrong sensitiveness which is so very involved with myself and not with others. That is a mold. But under that is again a vein of gold: a sensitivity, a concern that, turned out upon others, would be a great sensitivity for the glory of God, for the cause of God, for the Church, a great suffering sensitivity when our Mother the Church is wounded, that delivers us from looking at our real or supposed personal wounds. There would be a wonderful sensitivity to pour out upon the suffering, unflagging Vicar of Christ, whose words are so often disregarded, rejected, despised. There is the gold; and our Lady's coming and standing, so to speak, in our prayer on that moldy rock of sensitiveness can turn it to the gold of sensitivity for God and Holy Church and the millions of suffering, aching people in the world who are especially committed to our care.

The third rock I would put before your consideration and your prayer is a jagged rock, full of points. And that, I think, is readily comparable to impatience: if everything doesn't go right as I consider it right, I make a lot of noise about it. I am irritable. Things must be what I consider right—right now. This must be changed right now, this person must do differently right now, and I am very impatient at any obstacle to my plans. But under that jagged rock of impatience, of force, is again a vein of gold—if that force is for the coming of the Kingdom of God, if I have a holy impatience for it. I want to use all the strength of my prayer, of my self-giving, of the opportunity for sacrifice that God puts before me, that his Kingdom may come. If I am not burning with holy impatience that his

Kingdom should come in my own heart, how can I pray that it comes in the world? And so, again, we invite our Lady to come and stand on that jagged rock of our quick impatience and turn it to gold, to make it a holy impatience for the coming of the Kingdom.

I leave it to each of you to look for rocks in your spiritual lives and to ask our Lady to come and to turn them to gold. At Tepeyac she didn't take away the rocks; she did something more wonderful: she stood on them and she turned them to gold. And so—whether it be the black, sooty, muddy rock of discouragement, with its vein of gold to do better; whether it be the moldy rock of self-absorbed sensitiveness, with its vein of gold of sensitivity for God and his Holy Church and all the suffering people of the world; or whether it be the jagged rock of an impatience that will not wait, but under which there is the vein of gold of holy impatience for the coming of the Kingdom—let us ask our Lady to come and stand on our poor, old rocks and to turn them to gold with her presence.

✤ ✤ ✤ ✤

MONDAY OF THE SECOND WEEK OF ADVENT

Faith, Hope, and Love

*When Jesus saw their faith he said, "As for you, your sins
are forgiven"* (Lk 5:20).

MY DEAR SISTERS, today in the Gospel our Lord praises the
faith of those who lowered the paralytic through the roof
so that Jesus could heal him. Let us continue to reflect on
the theme we had in the Sunday readings of giving evidence that we wish to reform our lives, and let us examine
the evidence of our own willingness to be healed, which
pertains to faith, hope, and charity. *To reform* literally
means, not to make a new form, but to go back to the
original form. The Cistercian abbot Dom Gabriel Sortais,
O.C.S.O., said, "Our Lady was exactly as God dreamed
her." She never had to be reshaped; the form never had to
be reintegrated. Unfortunately, we often need to be reshaped and reformed. Yet that, too, is beautiful: that we
are formed again, not in a different way, but back to that
dream (a lovely expression) that God has of each one of
us, that dream-form in the mind and the heart of God of
what he intends each of us to be. This is what we mean by
reform.

Faith, we are told in Scripture, is the substance of things
unseen. It is easy to say, "I believe in God." But to say
that "I believe that God is in control" can be very hard—
to really give him the evidence of the heart, of the soul
bowed down before him, sometimes in confusion at what
he seems to be doing (and not doing) and sometimes in

real anguish—and to believe. This is the evidence he is asking of us. We tend to think of faith as a lovely thing. Faith is not just a matter of speaking, but it is a matter of believing when it is difficult to believe.

Our Lady at the Annunciation had to ask for some light on the subject: How shall this be? She did not doubt, but she didn't really know just how to believe this. And so she asked. In puzzlement, in bewilderment, and perhaps most of all in anguish, when it seems like things are not going right, when it seems almost like God has lost control—this is the hour of faith, not perhaps when the head is lifted and smiling, but when the head is bent in bewilderment, in anguish. God asks us now in Advent to give evidence of our reform, of our being formed again into the essence, the radicality of "I believe"—not because I see, but because I don't see.

Then there is the evidence of hope that we give him. Saint Claude de la Colombière, the apostle of hope, said: "I hope, and I will always hope. And I will never cease hoping. When it is clear that there is no longer any reason to hope, then I will hope all the more." That caught my heart, my mind, when I was very young. But in his determination to give all his anxieties over to God, even he had to discover, as we do, that this is very hard to accomplish. We do not really want to let go of them. They are debilitating, they are degenerative of our forward action, and yet it can be very hard to let go of our anxieties. We ask: "But how is it going to turn out? It is getting more confused all the time; the skeins are more tangled all the time." Hope is such a strong thing, because it is hope in the face of almost everything not presenting human reason for hope. Where shall God ask for evidence of this hope if not among his contemplatives? Dom Gabriel, speaking about faith and hope and love in prayer, said that when a contemplative is crushed with anxieties and still hopes, this man is praying. How I love that. It can seem sometimes that one can hardly formulate a prayer, but one hopes on. This man, he said, this monk, is praying.

Then, the evidence of love: realizing more and more that love is perhaps less lyric than dogged. Love, true love, will not give up; love goes on loving and loving. In the end, if it is really lyric, it is only because it has been persistently dogged; it will not give out. Faith, hope, and love, of course, are so closely intertwined.

The liturgy says, "He will appear", and adds, "at last". This is connected very precisely to what we have just been saying. We are all like the watchman on the tower, the sentinel watching and waiting. Scripture doesn't say that Jesus will appear at any minute but that "at last" he will appear, and that we can count on this "because he is true to his word". We ask ourselves, when perhaps many things seem to be tangled (and increasing in this state all the time), do we believe that he will appear at last? Do we believe it, not because of what we see, but just because he is true to his word? In one of the antiphons at Vespers we heard the familiar words: "Have courage, all of you, lost and fearful." We want to linger on these wonderful words. Sometimes we can feel as though we are the only ones who ever got this lost, the only ones who ever had so many fears pressing in upon us! But these words were written quite a while ago: "Have courage, all of you, lost and fearful." We are lost every time that we allow our faith, our hope, and our love to weaken. Then, of course, we are fearful. The antiphon goes on to say, "Take heart, and say: 'Our God will come to save us.'" He will come to save us—in the great act of redemption, yes, but also in the situations that seem too much for us.

We had in yesterday's oration: "Remove the things that hinder us from receiving Christ with joy." What are the things within me that hinder me from receiving Christ with joy? Do they not have a common denominator, that there is some lack of faith, some wavering of hope, some weakness in love? Where is my faith weak? Where are the loose threads in my hope? Where is the weakness in my love?

I ask you to take these few simple words and knead them into your thoughts, to take them into your own prayer. We want to be determined, with God's grace—which will not be lacking, which is superabundant in this season—to give him evidence of our allowing him to reform us to his original thought of us, his original dream of us, so that we really are women of faith, which is a suffering thing; of hope, which is a demanding thing; and of love, which is a dogged thing, so that it can become lyric.

TUESDAY OF THE SECOND WEEK OF ADVENT

Wide Open Gates

MY DEAR SISTERS, how many riches of Advent we could share here together. As I have searched among them our dear Lord stopped me at that great word of Advent, which we will be praying again and again, the watchword of Advent, "Come!" Now there are two elements in "Come!" and I think this is the whole spirit of Advent: it is a season of quiet—a season of folded wings—and anyone coming into the monastery should know that this is the Advent season. There is a hush upon the life; there is a folding, indeed, of the wings of the spirit, of the heart, in prayer; there is a low-hummed tenderness of the season that is part of "Come!"

And then there is also a great urgency. It is not that we fold our wings and just rest. We do rest in prayer; we enter into the hush of what is happening, what the Church is again putting before us, and the growth of Jesus within us. We cannot bring him forth if he does not grow within us; we shall bring forth only ourselves; our words shall be like the tinkling of cymbals, as sounding brass, and our actions will be just a great flurry of busyness, or, at the other end of the spectrum, the slow-footedness of sloth. So there is also this great urgency to do, and both of those things are present in "Come!"—are they not? It is the expression of desire and of permission. When we say to a person, "Come!" it is a desire. We do not honestly say, "Come!" to a person or to a thing that we do not desire. The second element is the permission. We have to let the person in. This is what we mean by "Come!": desire and permission. We must desire our Lord to come into our lives, and that "Come!" must be wholehearted. "Come! Come! I want you."

But then we have to permit him to come as he is. This can be seen on parallel planes: the coming of God into our lives, and the sisterhood. We do not say to Jesus, "I desire you to come, but I do not permit you to come as you are. Don't come with your wounds, don't come with your suffering, don't come as you are." We have to open wide the gates and permit him to come. He does not storm the gates. He says in Holy Scripture, "Behold, I stand at the gate and knock. And anyone who lets me in, I will sit down, and I will take my repast with him" (Rev 3:20). He has to be let in. It is not some kind of vague, nebulous "Come", but it is a real opening of the gates and allowing him to come as he is. We cannot say, "Yes, come, but do not come bringing the will of the Father; I might not like that. Do not come with your wounds. Do not come with what you will ask of me. Do not come with any of your demands: that if something offends me, I should just turn the other cheek; that if something is taken away from me, I should see if there is anything else that I could give besides." This *is* the kind of thing he comes with, and we cannot have that element of desire, unless the element of permission is there.

We see this same thing in the sisterhood. We cannot, in the growth and intimacy of the sisterhood, say, as it were, to any of our sisters, "Yes, come into our life, come into the sisterhood, but don't bring your personality, don't bring your temperament, don't bring your limitations, don't bring your eccentricities. Get rid of all these and then come." No, this would be a very unreal "Come!"

We say to Jesus, "Come! Come as you are—very poor." He is coming as a poor child; he is coming as a helpless child, needing his Mother's human love, his foster father's care for him, and our care for him as he grows in our spiritual life, as he grows within us. Our holy Mother Clare has said that just as the Virgin Mary carried him in the little cloister of her holy womb, so, too, we can carry him and bring him forth.

So, I ask you to take this very deeply into your prayer, so that we are not just facilely mouthing, "Come, come!" without realizing what we are saying. Then each "Come!" would ring very hollow in heaven. We want it to fill the world; we want to reach out to all the world, so that it says, "Come!" If we open wide, he will come in; he will grow within us, in each of our lives and in the life of our community, and we will be able to respond with joy to everything that his coming asks of us, expected, unexpected; ordinary or extraordinary; predictable or unpredictable. He will come in and give us the strength as he says, "I will take my repast with him; I will take supper with him, if he lets me in." Then we will be nourished unto the fullness of him whom we have allowed to come into our souls, whom we have allowed to come into us both in himself and through the sisterhood.

✤ ✤ ✤ ✤

Advent Overflow

Learn from me, for I am meek and humble of heart (Mt 11:29).

SAINT PAUL in writing to his beloved Thessalonians expressed his wish that they increase and overflow in love for one another. I want to linger on that "overflow" with you today. How does the little coming King teach us about overflow? I jotted down here four points.

It wasn't enough for him, so to speak, to come in humility. That humility had to overflow so that we would say, "How small can he be? How small can God be?" Now, he came in the Incarnation, of course, in the greatest miracle that could ever be: a baby who was a Divine Person born of a Virgin. We sing over and over, "*Natura mirante*"—the whole law of nature was stunned; nature was overwhelmed; nature was marveling. He could have done it a different way. It would also have been a miracle, if suddenly, like Melchizedek in the Old Testament, he had just appeared, "without forebears, without ancestors". Our Lord could have suddenly come into society. And would not this have seemed a better way to achieve his end? Nobody would have been able to shrug his shoulders and say, "Isn't he just the son of the carpenter? Isn't he just Mary's son? Where did he get all this?" If he had suddenly appeared as a grown man, another kind of miracle, we would have thought that this would have been a little more society-shaking.

But instead there was this overflow. In our poor little

human way of trying to express things, it is as though the Father looked over all possibilities of miracle by which his own second Person, the Divine Logos, would enter into human history, and takes the most impossible one, the humblest one of all. That's what I mean: How small can he be? A human embryo who is a Divine Person, who for months was not even visible in the form of his Virgin Mother. How small could he be? This is the overflow of the humility of God. Let us linger long on that in our prayer. And let this prayer actuate our own living: a little bit of humility is not enough. It must be total. And if it is to be rewarding, it must be total. It must not be occasional. It is for all the time. Because, as our Lord grew in the womb of his Mother, as he grew into boyhood, into manhood, into his public life, he took no respite from humility, to the end of his life. He had no days off. How small could he be? How humble could he be?

Then there is the overflow of his poverty. Again we ask, "How little can he have?" Even a poor baby does have some kind of a crib, is in some kind of a home. But he? How poor can he be? How little can he have? How much can he do without? And in the ripe years of his manhood, he will say, "I do not have any place to lay my head." He seeks hospitality sometimes at Bethany. But many times, surely, he must have slept under the stars. We know that at least once he slept in a boat. How little could he have? And how acquisitive we can be! Perhaps not of things, although we are certainly not immune from that, but how acquisitive can we be of the way things must be arranged, the time that decisions must be made, the way this must be done. And our Lord is saying to us in his overflow, "How little can you have? How much can you do without?" On the spiritual level, the level of my interior acquisitiveness, my interior concupiscence, how much can I do without? It is when we reduce our holdings to their absolute minimum, to relate to his overflow, that we are happiest. When I have to have my way, and I have to have this done right now, and this has got to be figured out right now, and this has got to be arranged— this is not when we are happy. We know that, yet we forget it very easily. So this, I think, is the second overflow. How little could he have? Just some straw, a little swaddling, a Mother, and the angels singing.

Then, dearest sisters, we look at the overflow of his meekness, and we say, "Just how patient can he be?" There was his life with those who didn't understand, those who contradicted him, those who during his Passion and even before that would treat him in a churlish way. How meek can he be? How patient can he be? We see his overflowing patience. Not in any of the Gospel incidents does our Lord say, "Well, I am really finished with lepers." But, just that very meek statement, "Didn't I cure ten people? Where are the nine?" Or, the very meek statement, "How long have I been with you; how often have I been saying these things and you still do not understand?" What a meek question! He is not pounding the table. But his meekness is overflowing, marvelously. Even at the Paschal meal, the last meal of his life with his apostles, when they are still squabbling, when they still can't really listen to him, he is so meek; he just goes right on. He gets down and washes the feet of these squabbling, contradicting persons whom he is going to love into martyrdom, love into greatness. And we look at this overflow and ask, "How meek can he be? How patient can he be?" And then we want to ask, "How patient can I be?"

And then the fourth overflow (and, of course, they are

all interrelated) is of his suffering love. I am sure we all love that line of the *Adoro Te Devote*, Saint Thomas' great hymn, which translates: "A single drop for sinners spilt is ransom for a world's entire guilt." The whole world. It doesn't even mean the present world. It means from the beginning of the world to the end of the world. Every Sunday, every solemnity, as I administer the precious Blood to you, always I am saying this in my heart, marveling: "A single drop for sinners spilt." Every drop in the chalice is super-sufficient, is ransom for the world's entire guilt, from the beginning of the world. Why didn't he just shed one drop? How loving could he be? How suffering could he be? Why did he do this? It is true that a single drop for all the sinners, from the beginning of time right down to the sinners in this room, is ransom for all our guilt. But, with him, it was, "How much blood? How much can I shed? How much can I do?" And it was to the last drop that he gave, so that even after death, when his side was pierced, the last drop came out. It was a sign of his suffering love. We ask: How many contradictions could our Lord suffer all of his life?—from those who would not make the effort to listen, those who were too obtuse to understand or who chose to be so, those who deliberately contradicted him. How long could he suffer? Well, right up to the end. They were still, in a sense, contradicting him at the Ascension, asking him, after all of this, "Now is the Kingdom? Our kind of kingdom: we sit on thrones, we get our way, we rule." How many contradictions, how many disappointments could he suffer? And the answer is: innumerable ones.

So, dearest sisters, we are truly splashed with the overflow of our Lord's giving. How small could he be? It is as though God searched for the smallest way so that we would get the message. How little could he have? How meek could he be? How much could his love suffer? We are called by the Church very directly in the words of the Apostle to "overflow in love". It can never be: "This will suffice. I give this much service, I give this much mercy, I give this much forgiveness, I give this much putting away of my own hurts, my disappointments, even the some-times-almost-bitter ones." How often will I put these away? There are *his* answers. We know that when a re-ceptacle for any liquid is filled to the brim, you cannot expect to move it without spilling some. And that is a wonderful thing spiritually. Because if we are really over-flowing with love for one another, we cannot move with-out its splashing out. We can't work, we can't recreate, we can't sing, we can't chant, we can't pray, we can't do any of these things, if we are really overflowing with love for one another, without its splashing over. So, let us try, dearest sisters, to have our sisters and the whole monastery splashed with the overflow, and the whole Church splashed with our little overflow, and the Holy Father himself splashed with our overflow. Let us be intent on this. Come now, let us begin. And let us keep that mea-sure so full of love, because this is not beyond us. We cannot all of us perform Herculean works of penance. We cannot and need not produce brilliant works of mind or artistry. But we can all be overflowing with love, every one of us, so that we just can't move without splashing it over the house, over our sisters, over the Church.

✣　✣　✣　✣

THURSDAY OF THE SECOND WEEK OF ADVENT

Great Moments

Among those born of woman there has been none greater than
John the Baptist (Mt 11:11).

DEAR SISTERS, I was very struck by the thought our homilist shared yesterday. Getting right to the heart of things, he said, "There are times when we don't feel like praying, and we pray. There are times when we don't feel like doing our chores, our work, and we do it. And *that's* holiness." And then he talked also of the really great moments in our lives. This is the theme for this brief sharing with you.

So often we miss the great moments in our lives. Perhaps we are thinking of the great thing to happen or the great decision to be made, the great step to be taken. But sometimes we miss the really great moments that are interior, as Father brought out in his very simple, homespun examples. For the very great moments of our lives are always very simple.

We think of the martyrs. Their holiness lies not so much in the moment when they approached the executioner's block to be decapitated for the love of Christ and for the Faith, as in all the hidden moments when perhaps the heads of their plans, their hopes, their trust, had been cut off. Those were the hidden moments of choice that they would go on. Before any martyrdom, dear sisters, many little martyrdoms have gone before. It is the result of many previous choices.

Let us each look deeply into our own lives, and see what great moments we have perhaps missed. We will undoubtedly discover some great and hidden moments that brought us so much closer to Christ, to our Beloved. Examples are ready and accessible. Perhaps there was a time when we depended on someone for understanding, and thought, "This is the very place where I shall find understanding", but found it was not there. At that moment the inner decision was made: "Will I grieve?" Well, yes. But: "Will I feel sorry for myself? Will I rest in disappointment, or will I choose to understand that this is our Lord calling me to find perfect understanding only in him?" That would be a great moment in one's life. Or perhaps our expectations were confounded when we sought to set down our roots in something human, something beautiful, but something not spiritually as far as God was asking us to come. And this became an invitation to go forth to—I do not want to say "loneliness of spirit"— but to that aloneness which for all of us is necessary for a profound intimacy with Christ, who alone perfectly understands us. Another ready example would be a wound that we thought all healed, that wants to rip open again. And there comes the moment of decision whether we will investigate that wound again, allow ourselves to feel the rawness of it again, or whether we will simply and resolutely stitch it closed again. These are the great moments of life, where we really move forward into intimacy with our Beloved. I want you to summon up from your own life your awareness of these moments, and also to search for the great moments that you have let pass. They are never the great outward decisions. They are always the little inward decisions. We love to quote the saying of Augustine Cardinal Mayer, O.S.B., that "nothing great is ever achieved without suffering", but we need to believe it. And to believe that the heart is never really purified for Christ to take complete possession until many hidden martyrdoms of the heart have been undergone.

Let us reflect and pray deeply upon the great moments of our lives. What we do or do not do with them makes all the difference. The poem "The Great Refusal", by John Bunker, about the choice that one man made, comes to my mind. Thinking that it would be a little easier, he chose not to face the complete purification of the heart, the aloneness of spirit before God. The poem ends: "Yet by the fine irony of the unforeseen, the path he chose became for him indeed the difficult way of pain and loneliness that leads to God knows whither." We too have our choices to make. We have the great moments of our lives brought before our own tribunals, so to speak. So often we wait for the great decisions, the great hour, the great thing. The really great moment of interior choice is passing, and sometimes lost.

A final word, as you look into your hearts and search out these things. When you go over the times that, by God's grace, you have recognized the moment of choice and responded to it, you will remember that there was an inner joy that cannot be described. It can only be experienced—the joy of having made that choice not to let the rawness of an old wound reopen, of not sinking down over a lack of understanding just when you were sure you had it, or of any of these other things. You will remember that, after that choice, in that purification, you felt very beautiful. That, I think, in these little martyrdoms of the heart is the little crown of martyrdom, in which we derive peace from our great moments.

✣ ✣ ✣ ✣

Happy Struggles

*The Lord is coming from heaven in splendor to visit his people,
and bring them peace and eternal life.* —Entrance antiphon

MY DEAR SISTERS, the days are hurrying on. We want to look into what these days will hold. Without any doubt they will hold many, many graces for all of us. One could venture to say that God can hardly wait to offer us opportunities to grow closer to him. We want to see how he is saying in everything he asks of us, "Come", and we want to say, "Yes, I'm coming."

The liturgy says, "Let us cleanse our hearts for this coming." We know that this is in a normal woman's heart: something great is going to happen; it is Christmas; we've got to clean house. That's a beautiful urge, a womanly urge, but the house of myself is what I really need to clean, and I know we all want to do that. So it is wonderful to find that in the Office, the inspired Word of God is saying that we must cleanse our hearts for his coming. We must look in the corners of them and cleanse them, and we must take care of any cobwebs that have gathered in our hearts.

Dear sisters, this came into my heart preparing for this chapter. We all want to suffer something for God, but we just can't understand why suffering makes us suffer. We can't seem to put these two things together. We know that no one can be really united to a suffering and crucified Master without being part of it, yet we are continually amazed that suffering causes suffering. The Fathers of the desert and the classic writers of earlier centuries refer to the whole spiritual life as the spiritual combat. We know, too, as the Scriptures say, that the violent take the Kingdom of heaven by storm (Mt 11:12). Heaven is carried away by the one who struggles for that great prize. Yet, we can't understand why we don't feel emotionally so great while we are struggling. It is so difficult for us to link to our actions what is conceptually very clear.

In these precious days, let us try with God's grace to clarify that in our hearts. We know things will come that surprise us. We do see, at least dimly, the primary goal of doing what God wants as the only thing worth doing. What are my plans worth if they are not God's plans for today? We take our drab human feelings that we all have sometimes—we feel cross—and we cannot press a button and change our human reactions, but we can agree to suffer them. We can agree to struggle; we can agree to feel this way. Then we can cope. Otherwise, dear sisters, we cannot cope. And what brings joy into the very struggle is to face it that, yes, this is a struggle, but I do want to reach the goal. I do know conceptually that it cannot be reached without struggle. My will is not supine; it is something I must divert from my own ideas, my own conclusions, my own desires, and really give them to God. I feel this wresting within me sometimes and that is where the real choices are rooted. In the inevitable struggles of life, the struggles to do God's dear will in whatever he asks of us— the struggles against feeling despondent, the struggles against feeling discouraged, the struggles against feeling frustrated—let us allow ourselves to find the joy in them: this is what I want to suffer, what I will to suffer. It isn't an emotional joy. It's much deeper than that. It is the joy of the will. We read in the Scriptures: "For the sake of the joy set before him, he chose the cross" (Heb 12:2). And then the Cross became the joy.

And so, dear sisters, let grace triumph in these struggles. God holds out the grace; he will be holding out grace after grace to us in these days ahead. But he doesn't force his grace upon us; he offers it, and it is up to each one of us to reach out for it to take it, or to let it be lost. He will not force us.

What do we expect may come to us in these days that we want to make so precious? Great emotional élan every day? There will be some probably, but it will not be every day; it won't be twenty-four hours a day. We want a sense of self-satisfaction; well, sometimes what our little self is clamoring for is not satisfied, and it is such a good thing that it isn't. What about Jesus? Do we think that, in all the great sufferings of his agony and death and also in those little sufferings of every day, he always felt great emotional élan? He was human, too; he had stronger emotions than any of us because he was perfect, and his whole emotional system was fine-tuned to perfection. And so, he had these desires.

We think about our Lady on the way to Bethlehem. Do we really think deeply enough about what she suffered? And about Saint Joseph's suffering? How do we think he felt to take her off in her condition of expectancy, riding the mule to Bethlehem? Her heart must have been tempted to question, "Why is this?" And surely his heart was tempted to question. Neither was supine; these were real people.

There are struggles asked of us, as were asked of them. And the answer is faith. We will see later on, of course, in the Scriptures, that it says very plainly that she didn't understand what Jesus said to them after those three days' loss. And she asks him, "Why did you do that?" Those words, in a sense, sum up her whole relationship with the Son of God, who was the Son of her womb. And he gives her an answer that she doesn't understand at all. He says to all of us, in a different place in the Scriptures, "What I am doing you cannot understand now, but later you will understand." That is a precious thought to hold in our hearts. How many times we say, "I just don't understand this", and he says, "One day you will understand."

In the inevitable struggles of life—and the struggles of these special days—we don't need to understand. We just need to respond, and then to hear him say, "One day you will understand. One day I will explain everything to you—except, when that day comes, you won't need to ask."

Peace, and happy struggles.

* * * *

The Joy of Being Forgiven

O Shepherd of Israel, hearken, from your throne upon the cherubim, shine forth (Ps 80:2).

MY DEAR SISTERS, very likely all of you find it as difficult to believe as I do that tomorrow is Gaudete Sunday. We have arrived at the midpoint of Advent, and this great season of grace is half-spent. What have we done with it? What evidence have we given when we were called before the Church's tribunal in a very particular way in this second week, which depended on how much we lifted up our souls in prayer the first week? The Church knows that her children have not all turned in such a marvelous performance. And so we would expect that on the third Sunday of Advent the Church would say: You had better watch out. And in a sense she does. But her first word is: *Gaudete!* Her first word is: Rejoice! She is not telling us to rejoice, surely, in a shallow, superficial sense of, "Oh, well, that's life. People are weak and that's the way it goes. And so I don't have to worry; I am doing the best I can." But no, her joy, the joy that she puts before us and the summons to joy which she gives us, is something all bound up—inextricably bound up—with a sense of our sinfulness.

The liturgy of this coming Sunday is so joyful that that has become its name—Joy Sunday—*Gaudete* Sunday. The Church puts on her rose-colored vestments, and she says, "Play the organ; let's put the flowers back on the altar.

Rejoice!" Why? Because we are so in need of redemption, because hopefully our sense of our sinfulness and our misery has deepened. He who is coming is going to remedy all that.

On Joy Sunday, in a very particular way, there is put before us again and again the call for us to realize our need. A wonderful way for you to expand your prayer and to deepen it on Gaudete Sunday would be to search for these calls in God's word. How does the Church begin? In the very first reading, she says: "Rejoice! Let your joy overflow." We could stop right there for a moment. When joy is the real joy of God, given only to the humble person who knows herself so in need of forgiveness, then that joy always overflows. The joy of the humble cannot be contained; it always overflows. That is why the Church says: "Rejoice! And let your joy overflow."

Then she gives us the word of our Redeemer: "I am coming" . . . for what? Did he say, "I am coming to be your King. I am coming to solve all your problems. I am coming to make everything just so pleasant for you"? He says, "I, the Lord, am coming to save you." And who needs to be saved? Those who are greatly at fault. The more we are at fault, the more we need to be saved. And the more we realize we are at fault, the more we reach out for salvation. He says: "I am coming to save you." We, no less than his first community of apostles, have a much more impoverished idea of his coming. We may think: He is coming to crown us. He is coming to equalize all the materialities of the world. We would like that. We would like no one to be deprived. And we would be an anomaly of humanity if we did not. But this is not really what he is coming to do. He is coming to teach us how to suffer, because we know our need of being saved. He is not coming to empty all the hospitals and to raise all the dying from their deathbeds and to establish an economic level and to make all things politically just and right. He is not coming to solve our President's problems, or our Holy Father's, at one great sweep. He is coming to save us. And that is what we rejoice about. The more we recognize our need to be saved, our need to be forgiven, then the more we rejoice and the more it overflows. May I say it again: the joy of the humble can never be contained.

Then he goes on to say, "I will free you from your sins." Sometimes we can be thinking, "What sins? I am doing my very best, and I wish some other people would, too." Of course, we smile when it is put that crudely, and yet we know that element can be in us. We can have a sharp eye for the faults of others and such a blind eye for our own. There is always that inverse ratio. But he is coming to free me from my sins, and each of you from your sins, and our community from our corporate sins, and our Church in America from its weaknesses, and the whole company of the Church from its human limitations. He is coming to save us. And certainly no one wants to say, "Who, I?" We want to be there. "I am coming to save you."

Then the oration says, "May we experience the joy of salvation", that is, the joy of being forgiven. Sometimes we find a difficulty within ourselves to rejoice in being forgiven. And yet, surely, all of us have experienced sometimes that joy, and we must keep a good memory for it: that we were really happy when we were rejoicing that God forgave us—the marvel of it. His priest said, "I absolve you from all your sins." He didn't say, "Well, you don't have any." He said, "I free you from all of them. God, through my lips, forgives you." Then there is the joy of being forgiven by our sisters. Yet at other times there is this ugly, polluted tide that rises within ourselves that we do not wish to be forgiven, because we do not want to admit that we are so in need of being forgiven. So we find fault with others, we find fault with situations, we find fault with circumstances, we find fault with the way things were effectuated or actuated. Then we miss the whole point. We become more and more spiritually myopic about seeing our need to be forgiven, and we set ourselves right outside the liturgy and the truth.

Then there is that other expression of pride which forgives from a height: "I am *not* the one at fault, but, yes, I reach out to forgive *you*, you poor creature." This never avails. We forgive standing together on the level of our sinfulness. During the general confession of faults at chapter, I looked down and saw that happily there are many little sinners all kneeling together. It is such a beautiful sight, such a beautiful picture of community. There is nobody standing upright and saying: "I don't belong to this group, so I had better step out in front." But we are all huddled very closely together because we are all so in need of forgiveness. That is what little sheep do. They huddle very close together in their common needs, in their small quarters. And so we huddle together in community with that great bond of our all needing to be forgiven, that we may experience that joy of being forgiven, that joy of salvation.

And then the liturgy goes on to tell us that "he comes with power and might". Again, to do what? To make all things egalitarian? To level off all things, to solve all problems, to end all suffering? No, it says he comes with power and might to save. That is the great power. That is the whole mystery, is it not, of the Incarnation; that is what he came for—to save us. He did not come just to be the darling Child in the crib, but he came with the sign of the Cross already upon him. Chesterton says that, whereas other people are born into the world to live, Christ knew he was born into the world to die.

The liturgy tells us again, "Let us cleanse our hearts that we may be ready to welcome him". This is the decoration of the heart, its cleansing: knowing its need to be forgiven. Then it goes on to mention some cures that there will be, if we admit humbly our need to be forgiven and rejoice in it. We recently read again that dread prophecy in Isaiah, where he sends his prophet, as it were, on a great mission of failure, to speak to the ears that will not hear and to the eyes that will not see. But now he says that they are going to be cured, if they *want* to be cured. The liturgy says: "On that day the deaf shall hear . . . and the eyes of the blind shall see." Isn't that wonderful? Because we know (and we want to know it better) we are often so deaf to God's call to greatness, to God's alert to the opportunity to grow in sacrificial love, so blind to his goodness—and sometimes so blind to the goodness in one another because we are looking at the blemishes, and we do not have the vision to see the goodness. But if we are right in the front rank saying with Saint Paul, and perhaps challenging Saint Paul's right to say, "I am the greatest sinner. I am the one who needs you most", then our ears will begin to hear and our eyes to see. This is the mystery of Christmas, the beginning of redemption.

And so with the rest of the liturgy, with the themes that are common to all the Sundays and to all the days: the leveling of the mountains of pride within us; the making straight of these winding, tortuous, devious ways within us. This will be done by God, if we come humbly admitting we cannot do it ourselves. We cannot level these mountains within us. And we cannot excuse ourselves from our inability by looking at real or supposed mountains in others. We cannot straighten out the paths or smooth the rough ways within ourselves if we are occupied with others' real or supposed rough measures. We take our place as the ones who so need to be forgiven and who so rejoice to be forgiven, without the proud attitude of: "What do I need to be forgiven about? What about her? What about these other things?" Then we arrive with God's grace at that knowledge of our need to be forgiven—and come to rejoice in it. Isn't this marvelous that God really puts up with me? Surely each of us wants to say that: it's a marvel.

In our really happiest moments we marvel that our sisters put up with us. We make good resolutions, and we break them. We want to be patient, and we are impatient. We are sharp, sometimes; we are ungenerous; we are lazy; we are overbearing; and we are critical. Then we let God's grace operate in us, and we can rejoice in marveling that our sisters put up with us. People who have this state of mind are happy people. The unhappiest in all this world must be those who think they have no need to be forgiven. These are also the most unforgiving people, the ones who, if they want to dole out supposed mercy, will do it from a height of pride, which is always destructive of themselves and wounding of others. So when the Church says, "'Rejoice!' again I say, 'Rejoice!'" we want to respond because we have understood the rest of the Church's message: that to rejoice we need to be cleansed for his coming; we need to be forgiven. And the great Forgiver, the great Redeemer, is on the way. May none of us ever deprive ourselves of this joy.

THIRD WEEK OF ADVENT

✤ ✤ ✤ ✤

THIRD SUNDAY OF ADVENT, YEAR A

True Rejoicing

MY DEAR SISTERS, it is more than a little difficult to believe that we have arrived at Gaudete Sunday, but this is so. Swiftly Advent goes, swiftly go the opportunities, swiftly go the graces. Now, everyone wants joy, wants to rejoice. If a person really loves to be glum, really enjoys being depressed, this is a very dangerous sign, because every human heart reaches out for joy. And so we sing today the marvelous words of Saint Paul, who tells us that we should rejoice always. Then he repeats it, the Latin text using the word *iterum*, which is a very strong word, translated, as best we can but really rather weakly, as "again". It carries much more force than that. If we would put it colloquially, we would say, "Now did you get that?" or "Get this now!"; or we could say of *iterum*: "Pay attention!" "Get this straight." So, "Rejoice always, *iterum*"— "I say it again, pay attention! Listen—did you understand? Rejoice always."

Perhaps many through the centuries (and we with them) have puzzled over how this can be in the inspired words of Scripture. Can we always rejoice? Can we look at our world so ravaged by war, so wounded in many areas by corrosive selfishness and riddled with drugs, alcohol, all manner of addictions, and say, "Rejoice always"? Then we look at the Church herself, our Mother, and we ask how she can say this to us when we see how she is suffering. How can we pray this, how can we sing this when we see the Church suffering so much from her own, so beleaguered by the pride of those who should be her most faithful members? Then we look into our own lives and see many things that are not cause for joy, and we say, how can this be? When we step back and look at the inspired writer himself, we may wonder how he could say that, he who was later to list for us carefully how many times he was shipwrecked, scourged, criticized, and blamed.

This is an inspired word of Scripture, but it cannot be clear, it cannot even make sense if we leave out the words *in Domino*. This little prepositional phrase, *in Domino*, alone explains it all. Saint Paul wasn't as happy as he could be that he was hunted down, that he was flogged, that many people were plotting his death, that many did not listen to him, that many mocked him, and that he had disagreements and lack of understanding with his own, that he was imprisoned, hungry, and cold, often deserted by most; but *in Domino* Paul had learned the profundity of *gaudete*, and that gave him the right to be God's instrument in proclaiming to us, "Rejoice always; I say it again, rejoice always in the Lord."

Then we look at our Mother the Church. Why isn't she mourning at all that is happening now? She grieves, yes, but in the Lord she rejoices. All through the centuries, all through two thousand years, the Church has never yet said, "No Gaudete Sunday this year." Never. And she has been through very hard times, even harder than ours, and always she has said, "Rejoice always in the Lord", in whom she rejoices because she belongs to him. She is his Bride. How do we call the Church to rejoice? Not in any way but *in Domino*.

Let us look a little more at joy, now that we know with all finality where it is situated, *in Domino*, in order to find how we get there. We cannot rejoice totally in things, in others, or in myself. But we rejoice in faith. And the stronger the faith, the greater the rejoicing. Let us consider these three places where so often we try to find joy: first, *in rebus*, in things. There is something in all of us, that if this were different, oh, how I could rejoice. If this circumstance were changed, if I had different work to do, if I had more time, if I had more this or that or the other thing, oh, I would be so joyful. We shall never find real joy *in rebus*, but when the joy is *in Domino*, then *in rebus* it multiplies. No longer dependent on things, we discover how many things there are in which to rejoice; whereas if we try to situate our joy there, things will always betray us.

Then, we try to find joy in others. Things fail us as an enduring source of joy, and others fail us. This also must be. Others give us much joy, but just as things are so ephemeral, so also persons, all of us, are so unpredictable. And sometimes when we look for joy in persons in whom we have been quite convinced we would find it, we find that, unpredictably, they give us something else. Again this is God leading us forward, for although we do indeed receive much joy, and a greater joy *in personis* than *in rebus*, this cannot be on what we depend. God will allow that they will fail, because he is always leading us to *in Domino*. But the more our joy is rooted and situated in him, the more we will find to rejoice us both in things and in others. This is a wonderful paradox: that it is not that we put aside things as joy-givers but that we put them aside as the source of our joy. It is certainly not that we feel disappointed in persons and put them aside as a cause for our joy. No, it is that we go beyond that to the One who will never fail us, who is not ephemeral. "O God unchangeable and true", we sang each day in a hymn of the Divine Office during the first years of my religious life: *immotus in te permanens*, the unfailing One, the always predictable One as concerns being our strength and our joy.

It is the person most rooted in joy who sees the most beauty in things, who perhaps gets the most excited about little things. Look at our Holy Father Francis. Certainly he was rooted *in Domino*. He was not trying to find his joy in things, but because he found it in the Lord, he found more joy in a day than most men or dozens of men together found in all their lifetimes. It all depends on what is in the primary place. And so with persons. Francis loved more and more and more persons, and though he received great sorrow from many of them and doubtless multiple little disappointments, he greatly rejoiced in persons. "The Lord gave me brothers." And though these brothers were sometimes not so outstanding for their fidelity and their understanding, he rejoiced that God gave him brothers. It was always in God, always *in Domino*.

So, it is faith in the Lord that gives us joy, faith that the Lord really knows what he is doing. And once we are empirically convinced of that, practically convinced of that, when the faith is real and burning, then it is no longer necessary that we should understand. It is enough to be certain in faith that God understands exactly what he is doing. And we rejoice. Who could not rejoice *in Domino* to know that this is our God and that he knows what he is about?

Sometimes we try to find our joy in figuring things out, finding a way out or in, or in and out of things, but our real joy is *in oratione*, in bringing everything to him in prayer, being convinced that God knows exactly what he is doing even though this is often not at all clear to us. It is intensely interesting that in this same short passage the Apostle (out of so much travail, personal and ecclesial) is saying, "Rejoice in the Lord all the time", and then immediately goes on to say, "In prayer make all your needs known to God." It is not that we say, "God knows exactly what he is doing and he knows everything so I just sit back and make my act of faith." No, God wants us to tell him over and over again what our needs are. *Innotescant*, he says; "make them known" to God. I wonder if we ponder enough on the spiritual charm of that. "Go and tell God what he already knows", is what the Apostle is saying. Tell him all about the things that he is completely aware of. God wants to be told by us the needs that he knows much better than we ever could. And he invites us in this inspired word of Scripture to do just that. So, if you want to rejoice, you must have faith; it must be *in Domino*. But then you must pray and you must keep telling him of your need. And you must keep bringing your poverty before him and your failures before him and your disappointments before him and your heartaches before him, all the time: *Semper in oratione innotescant petitiones tuas*—tell him all your petitions. It is wonderful, isn't it? That is the second point, that in all things we must use all our own faculties and powers, but with an understanding always of our limitations and our insufficiencies—and with a loving acceptance of the limitations and insufficiencies of others, because it must be so. If it were not, we might have many gods instead of one God.

Thirdly, there is trust. All three of these are very closely related, and trust might seem the same; but it is not quite the same as faith. Faith pertains to believing with all our hearts that it can be done. Trust is the assurance that it *will* be done. We have faith in God when we know that he can do all things for our good. And we trust him when we rest in the assurance that he will do all things for our good. When we say we have great faith in a person's abilities or a person's potential, we mean we have great faith in what this person can do. But trust is believing that the person *will* do it. There is a difference.

Again, this brings with it the abdication of anxiety. It is a very profound consideration that at Holy Mass the Our Father is always followed with a little prayer asking that we be protected from anxiety, because it is a destructive thing. We do not suffer purely when we are full of anxiety. This is something from which we must be delivered in order to rejoice always. It is trust, trust in God that delivers us from anxiety. Again we see the insufficiency of earth to fulfill the Word of God. We see that only God is sufficient to fulfill his promises. Then we rejoice because we know that he will do so. We do not know how, we do not know when, we do not even know if we will have the sense to see it, but we know that he will.

We want to meditate, to reflect, to immerse ourselves in the mystery of joy. All through the centuries, the philosophers have wrestled with this. If there is a good God, why is there all this pain, why is there this sorrow? But the joy is always *in Domino*. We don't know, but he knows. What we do learn is that he is drawing us all, he is calling us to know that there is really nothing stable outside himself, and that in him and in him alone is the explanation of all things. Already as we ponder things in this way we begin to experience a serenity coming into our very pain, whatever it may be, that this is an all-loving God who is reminding us where we are all going. We are all moving steadily step by step each day, moving with each tick of the clock toward this terminus. This is what he wishes to say to us: in him alone all find their home. Something begins to come into our stricken hearts, that we are all going home. The more we are *in Domino* on this earth, the more we are already at home.

The Church does not say, "No Gaudete Sunday this year", but she says, "Rejoice in the Lord." The world is in travail and in turmoil, but God says, "Rejoice in me, rejoice." There is pain and suffering and there is the temptation to anxiety and there are the disappointments, but there is God saying, "*In Domino* is all joy". Let us sing then with all our hearts, not just on Gaudete Sunday, but always; and let us dance under the wreath of eternity, that all joy is in God, and that when he disappoints us in the evanescence of ephemeral things, when he allows us to be disappointed in persons, when he allows us to experience such disappointment in ourselves, he is only saying what he told Paul to say to us: "*Gaudete in Domino.*"

THIRD SUNDAY OF ADVENT, YEAR B

Joyous Replies

MY DEAR SISTERS, surely with something of a gasp of wonderment, almost of unbelief, we find that we have come to Gaudete Sunday—Joy Sunday—and are approaching the beginning of the solemn Christmas novena. And we are, all of us, surely, a little giddy over the riches of the liturgy poured out upon us every day. The liturgy of Gaudete Sunday, taking us into the novena, will certainly not offer us less rich viands than we have been given these past first weeks of Advent. On what shall we reflect today, out of the many possibilities offered us? Certainly we can linger long on the first reading from the prophet Isaiah, who is saying to us that Jesus is coming, our Lord is coming, to bring glad tidings to the lowly. We don't want to miss anything of the glad tidings of his coming, of his redemption. So we need to be very earnest about aligning ourselves with the lowly, or nobody is going to hear anything.

We know how many don't hear. How many, not through their own fault, have never had the glad tidings preached to them. But how many have, and have not heard because they are not lowly of heart. We have, in our own time, so-called theologians who are professedly expert students and teachers of the Word of God—only they don't hear it. And what is the reason? Scripture tells us: God speaks to the lowly of heart. We want to be very concerned about that.

In the second reading, from Thessalonians, God says to

us through the Apostle Paul not simply, "Avoid evil; don't sin." He says, "Don't have anything to do with whatever even looks like this, even smells like this, even has the least odor of this, the least outline of this." He says, "Refrain from every kind of evil." If there is anything shadowy about this, if it is not really good, then have nothing to do with it, nothing at all. Avoid any semblance of evil. How is it that often we have to see ruefully (and, I trust, very contritely), that we have committed faults, that we have not responded to grace, that we have not made the sacrifices asked of us? It is not that we immediately went off hand in hand with this evil, but that we have lingered with the semblance of evil, wandered into those murky areas. Here is something generous to do, but have *I* really got time to do it? Should I be the one, *again*? Maybe somebody else instead? That is the semblance of evil, and it will take us right into it. Similarly, if after a correction we weigh it or think there is something to be explained away, that, too, is a semblance of evil and it will assuredly lead us into evil. We could go right down the list.

However, what I want especially to linger on is the holy Gospel from Saint John, in which he is talking about his friend with the same name, Saint John the Baptist. We have the familiar passage in which people are saying, "Who are you?" and then, "What do you have to say for yourself?" Let us see how these questions directed to Saint John the Baptist apply to us.

"Who are you?" Well, there is no question about this, no question at all, because this answer is God's to give. The answer is factual. It is deifically objective. God has the answer: You are the one I have wanted to be. You are this person who is a unique thought of mine, never again to be duplicated, never again to be thought. Who are you?

You are the one I thought worth redeeming, for whom I thought it appropriate (and one falls back in awe to use such a word, and yet it is correct, it is accurate) to deliver up to agony and death my only-begotten Son. That is who you are.

And then, who are you as a Poor Clare? You are the one whom I have called to a rare vocation, not because you deserved it but because I wanted it, I wanted you. I wanted you in this way, I wanted you in this intimate life of love with me, in this radical life. It is to you that I said, "I want you to die and your life to be hidden with my Christ, in me."

All these things, as I say, are deifically factual. That is who each one is. We cannot undo God's work: we cannot "unbaptize" ourselves, we cannot "uncall" ourselves, we cannot "unvow" ourselves. But what we can do is to obstruct the unfolding of our creation. What we can do is render inactive the graces of baptism. What we can do is render unavailing the effects of redemption. What we can do is to be unfaithful to our consecration. We do not need to linger unduly on these dark considerations, but they must be faced. They are terrible powers. We can obstruct the work of God, but we cannot undo, unravel, our identity. Who are you? This is who I am; this is the one for whom I will answer to God, and for whom no one else can answer for me.

But there is a second question: "What do you have to say about yourself?" This is a very searching question to put to ourselves, and answering it honestly will involve suffering, certainly, for all of us, because we all fail, we all fall, we have all been on occasion unresponsive. But it is a salvific suffering. God asks us, "What do you have to say about yourself?" This is a question each one of us must answer. And, oh, how wonderful, if we could each give Saint John the Baptist's answer: "I am the voice of one crying out in the desert, 'Make straight the way of the Lord.'" This would be truly to fulfill my creation, my baptism, my redemption, my call to the cloistered religious life.

Many questions, then, come out of this. In the wilderness of the world's wars and frictions and selfishness, am I really a voice crying out peace in every action of every day, in the peace I am always spreading and radiating in community, in the smoothing of the little frictions, the little irritabilities that are inevitable where human beings (especially a goodly number of them) dwell together? Am I never adding irritability to irritability, but bringing peace, smoothing the little situations, crying out in the wilderness? Am I a voice crying out sweetness and patience in the violence of the world? Violence seems to be multiplying on every side, in every nation including our own, and multiplied a hundredfold in the teeming cities of our country. In my daily living am I a voice crying out sweetness, gentleness? In the disunity and the fragmentation of the social units of the world, beginning with the basic one of the family, am I crying out a message of unity by my continual building of community? Am I crying out by my manner of living, "It is so good to suffer for unity, to humble myself so that unity may be preserved, to be always a healer, a binder"? Am I really the voice of my Beloved crying out all the time?

"What do you have to say of yourself?" Do I have to say that, sometimes, in the wars and the frictions of the world, I cry out irritability? Do I have to say that sometimes in the lack of peace in the world, I cry out impatience and selfishness? Do I sometimes have to say that in the divisiveness and the disunity of society, of the family, I cry out: me, me, me? This is the common denominator of all disunity, of all fragmentation.

These are very deep and searching questions. "Who are you?" We cannot undo who we are, we cannot pretend that we are not great, we cannot pretend that we are not called to the fulfilling of that greatness, to serve the ongoing creation of God in one another. We cannot deny that we have been redeemed, and at what a price. "You have been purchased", Scripture says, "at a price" (1 Cor 7:23). We cannot undo the fact that we are loved by God, and we cannot "shrug off" the responsibility of being loved, of being wanted, of being ambitioned by God to be holy.

Our dear Lord wants to help us with these questions and with these answers. He says to us, "The first question I have answered", and we know the answer. Now we work at the second question, so that we can truly say with Saint John: "I am the voice of one crying out in the desert, 'Make straight the way of the Lord.'" I am saying to the whole world: make straight the way of peace by each one being a peacemaker. The way you make it a generous world is by the little acts of generosity, and perhaps most especially by the little hidden victories over selfishness. The way that one clears up wildernesses in the Church herself, in some of her members, is by being lowly of heart and lively in faith and obedient. What my Mother the Church tells me, this I do, without question. Where she leads me, there I go. This is my ambition, to be that voice, the voice, which, in our weakness, will sometimes get off-key, sometimes drop in pitch, but which knows its theme, which knows its motif.

Each day may we more truly be to the world little voices of peace, of gentleness, of sweetness, of unity. As we celebrate Gaudete Sunday, I think that is the explanation of joy. Saint John was so happy to be a voice saying always, "There he is." This is what we are all called to be, and called in a particular way from the cloister, to be this to all men—not just to this or that certain group—but to all the world. And so, may we develop a very firm voice that gets truer and truer because it reaches all through the world.

✤ ✤ ✤ ✤

Third Sunday of Advent, year c

Happenings

MY DEAR SISTERS, recently we listened to a taped address in which the retreat master spoke about the evangelization that we are required to do in our contemplative life in relation to the little things of daily life: the little responses, the little interior victories that we are given the grace to achieve. He said that either we do it or we do not do it; but that, in one way or the other throughout the world, "something happens". It is about happenings that I want to speak to you today.

Often we have reflected together on the Mystical Body and that this is not a devotion but a doctrine, something that the Church says you must believe, because this is the truth. We do affect one another throughout the whole Church of God by everything we do or do not do. We affect first of all that local church which is our own community. So, indeed, "something happens". Every time that I happily submit to what I love to call "the nudgings of grace" within us, something happens in the community. Each other sister is somehow strengthened by this. And when I do the opposite, putting God's dear, loving, summoning will aside for my own "reckless-driver" will, something also happens, something that would have been better not to have happened. We should have a great sense of our importance. What I do makes good things happen or withholds them from happening.

Today's liturgy for Gaudete Sunday is full of happenings. I had "happening" very deeply in my heart ever since

Father used that simple phrase on which he did not much expatiate, which seemed to me the more dramatic because of the quiet way he said it: "Something happens." A sense of responsibility has been with me on a very deep level ever since. When I looked at the liturgy, there it was: "happenings". These happenings that this Sunday's liturgy is talking about are our effects on other people. In God's teaching this Sunday he is telling us all about how we relate to others. In the joyous hush of Advent, the liturgy is not telling us: "Now, just be very hushed. Don't pay any attention to other people." Quite the opposite. In the first reading, the prophet Zephaniah is rather beside himself with the theme of joy. After his great outburst of "Shout for joy!" he says what is going to happen to us (the first happening) if we allow God to come. He says, "He will renew you in his love." What a wonderful thing this is! To be given God's own workshop in how to love more, that is the effect of joyous grace in our hearts: we are renewed in the ambition to love more, to do more for others. We are more driven by that need to love, to give, to serve. Then we turn this about and find that when we are renewed in love, we are much more joyful. Insofar as we are not reaching out love, understanding, service, mercy to one another, the less joyful we are. The most joyful person is always the most loving person. And the most lovingly given person is always the most joyful person.

In the second reading, from Saint Paul to the Philippians, we hear: "Rejoice in the Lord always! I shall say it again" (if you didn't hear me the first time), "Rejoice." And what is the result of that? There are various ways that you can translate *modestia*: humility, modesty. I prefer what the breviary translation uses: "Everyone should see how unselfish you are." Again, the result is joy; something happens. If I really rejoice in the Lord, then something happens. I am renewed in love. And when I am renewed in love and in that driving desire to love, to serve, to forgive, to understand, then something happens: I am more joyful. And when, as that passage in Philippians recommends, I am earnestly trying to deepen my prayer life, making everything known to the Lord rather than just playing a little record, and making things known to myself that had better be silenced, or sometimes trying to make things known to other people that I think they really ought to know, then I can rejoice in the Lord. And if you are really rejoicing in the Lord, everyone will see how unselfish you are; something will happen. Seeing unselfishness always invites us to unselfishness. Something happens for other people when we are unselfish. And when we are unselfish something happens to us.

In the Gospel pericope from Luke we have Saint John the Baptist preaching repentance to the people. When these different groups come to him, saying, "What are we to do?" he tells them to give and to serve, not to hurt anyone, not to withhold from anyone but to give. He says this to each group. Perhaps this is not what they were expecting, but how wonderful it is that he is explaining repentance that way. Something should happen in the way of doing what you have always been doing. It isn't that in this call to penance we go off to some dramatic new penance, but we do the same thing in a quite different way. Something happens. He says: "Now, if you have two coats, give one away. One coat is enough for you; that is all you can wear at one time anyhow. So give one away. That is what you should do, this is what I mean by a new life, this is what I mean by repenting." And if you have extra food, he doesn't say that you should starve yourself and give it all away but that you should share it, share it with others. Let something good happen for them. Never keep for yourself more than is really needed.

In a spiritual way, perhaps even more than in a material way, when we give away any excess, then we see excess better. The world in many places, and perhaps we in our own lives, can be so blinded by not giving of ourselves that we don't even realize—and that is a terrible punishment—that we have an excess. I keep for myself some time I could give away; I keep for myself some effort that I ought to give away; I keep for myself some strength that I should give away; I keep for myself the understanding that I should give to others. You can enlarge on that list. We all can.

The tax collectors come next and say, "What shall we do?" And Saint John says, "Don't cheat anybody." He doesn't say, "Go to another profession", but he says, "Do what you are doing in a different way, and don't cheat anybody." It is all about relationships: be renewed in love; let everybody see how unselfish you are; don't keep anything extra for yourself; don't cheat anybody. We say, "Can *we* cheat anybody?" Oh, yes, we know that we can cheat the community of the happiness that we must give it; of the joy that we should contribute to it; of the full service that we should give to it; of the mercy that we should give to it; of the compassion that we should give to each one in it.

Then the soldiers come, the colonels and the captains, and they say, "What shall we do?" Saint John says, "Do not practice extortion." He wants something to happen to them. Again, he is not saying, "Go to another profession" or "Step down from your position", but he says, "Do what you are doing in a different way. Don't be overbearing because you have this or that title, but invite others to do good. Invite others to obey." It is all about relationships, and allowing something to happen. We hope (and I think we can be pretty well assured) that because they asked honest questions, they went off and put to use his very honest answers. People who were storing up for themselves more than they needed really began to share it, to let something happen. We have good grounds for hope that the tax collectors (we would like to think all of them, surely some of them, we hope most of them) went off and decided that they would let something happen, too: that they would stop cheating, that they would stop looking out for their own interests at the expense of other people's interests. For when we look after our own interests so much, we are always cheating other people. Always.

We like to hope, and again I think we have very good grounds to hope, that the good colonels and the good captains and the good lieutenants went off and began smiling at people instead of frowning at them; began using an approach of "Why don't you do this?" instead of saying, "You do this or else!" When we have an attitude of "do this or else", usually people do decide to do "else".

So, dearest sisters, Advent is going on so swiftly, and things are happening. Grace is happening to us every hour. And we must let it happen, really let it happen—allow ourselves to be renewed in love; allow our sisters to see how unselfish we are. It is a beautiful vision. It is intriguing; you don't want to look away from it. You want to think, "I would like to be that good-looking myself!" It is wonderful. Something happens, to others and in ourselves. Let us look into ourselves and see where we are cheating the community a bit. Let us look into our own lives and see where we are overbearing or insisting, instead of inviting. And let us help one another to let grace "happen" within us.

❖ ❖ ❖ ❖

MONDAY OF THE THIRD WEEK OF ADVENT

Companionship

Come to us, Lord, and may your presence be our peace;
with hearts made perfect we shall rejoice in your companionship
forever. —Magnificat antiphon

Come to us, Lord, and bring us peace. We will rejoice
in your presence and serve you with all our heart.
—Communion antiphon

QUICKLY, quickly are these grace-fraught days passing. Out of the riches of the Advent liturgy, I would like to dwell particularly on that marvelous First Vespers antiphon of the Second Sunday, which is repeated in a somewhat different form in the Communion antiphon today. The Church puts into our mouths a most remarkable request: that Jesus come to us and bring us peace, and that we have companionship with him. Companionship is a very intimate and close thing. When we talk about companions we think immediately of those of one mind, of one desire, those who relate easily and happily to one another. Then, the *Magnificat* antiphon has us pray that the presence of Jesus would be our peace. I think we have here an excellent point of interrogation for ourselves. To what are we present? And does this presence bring us peace?

Surely we would all confess to our shame that sometimes we are present to things that we know very well have never brought us peace, and never will. We are present to busily nurturing a little hurt, a misunderstanding. We are present to memories that are better forgotten, although we are so slow to learn this. Or perhaps we are present to our own irritability. Such presences have never brought us peace. If we could just stop ourselves we would realize that being present to this memory, this incident, whatever it may be, is not making me feel peaceful. At the same time, we are in control of what we choose to be present to in our thoughts, in our hearts, in our ruminations—to what does bring us peace. When we think of how much we have been forgiven, of how much we have been given by our community, that brings us peace—because these things bring us a sense of humility, and humility is at the heart of peace. One could also say that peace is at the heart of humility. And we pray also that Jesus' presence may be our peace. He is always present if we allow him to be. We are certainly not always emotionally aware of his presence. Perhaps we find his presence only through embattlements, by casting out of ourselves what shadows his presence. But he always wants to be present and to give us the peace of his presence.

That wonderful antiphon then goes on to say that "with hearts made perfect", we can rejoice in his companionship. Surely we would all say we are quite far away from having perfect hearts. But what is the perfect heart? It is a humble heart. It is a grateful heart, is it not? I think a perfect heart could be defined as one that understands how unworthy it is to be loved and to be forgiven and to be wanted. All of these things are God's gift. There is no doubt that God loves us, that he has forgiven us many times and will always forgive us. There is no doubt about it at all. This is to have a heart made perfect: to know how unworthy we are of his love; but we have it! To know how unworthy we are to be forgiven again and again; but we are!

The antiphon comes to its climax by saying that we can rejoice in God's companionship. When we think of that word *companion*, we might think of two persons walking happily along, sharing confidences with one another, traveling along the road together. There is a very intimate companionship in traveling. The person is right there beside you all the time. Everything is done together. It is a situation of very great intimacy. This is what the Church is allowing us to ask for in this antiphon, that Jesus should be our companion. We want to rejoice in him just sitting there beside us, speaking to us very intimately, noticing things together with us on our way, praying together, supping together, being silent together, and interchanging together. This is a wonderful thing, to think of Jesus as being not only "the Way" but our companion *on* the way.

If companionship is the meeting of similarities, how can we be similar to Christ? He told us what he is like. He is love; that is God's name. He is meek and humble of heart. He is overflowing with mercy. So if we are to be his companions, and he ours, in our travel across the often turbulent waves of human existence, then we have to be all-loving and all-humble and all-merciful.

Other phrases in the liturgy serve this marvelous invitation to companionship. The prophet Baruch says that the mountains must be brought low and the age-old depths filled. There are things in us that have to be lowered before we can enter into that companionship, such as the little peaks of our pride. The phrase "the age-old depths" is another marvelous call to prayer. Let us ask, what are my age-old depths that need to be filled in? There are holes in myself that I dig out again and again, the little holes of self-pity or nurtured hurts at which I dig away. Baruch comes to tell us that these peaks need to be brought low and that these holes which we have dug in ourselves need to be filled in by Christ.

Some of the saints have aspired to be a slave of God; and that is a wonderful thing. To be a friend of God is what we want also. But to be a companion with him is even more intimate—we with him, and he with us as our traveling companion on the way to the Father. You don't mind the fact that maybe you're on turbulent waters or under a dark sky if you have a very intimate traveling companion. There is such a sense of well-being that comes with this. But what well-being could be comparable to having Jesus for one's traveling companion? And this is what he wants to be. Now, companionship is a duality; it is not just that he is a companion to me but also that I am a companion to him. Nobody can be a companion alone. What is being a good companion to him? He loves humility. He loves self-renunciation. He loves trust and he loves sacrifice. He loves utter giving to the other. This is how we prepare to be his companion. Let us be happily busy about that this Advent, as we think about being a companion to Jesus.

TUESDAY OF THE THIRD WEEK OF ADVENT

Joyful Penitence

MY DEAR SISTERS, in this third week of Advent following upon Gaudete Sunday, we find a deep call, a profound call, to the understanding of penance. I think the Church is trying to teach us that real penance is always characterized by joy, that joy is a property of penance.

When we look at penitence, we could perhaps list many properties, many characteristics and effects of penance; and we can all develop this in prayer. For today, I would like to linger a bit on three outstanding characteristics and effects of penance, three which I would venture to say are the most prominent. They are both property and effect; they are both descriptive of what is there and are a function of what is there. These three are: purpose, alertness, and joy. Now, when we really become aware of how much we need to do penance, of how much we have sinned and are at fault, we could question (if we look at it in a superficial way) how we could be joyful. Would we not grow sadder and sadder? But, no, this is not true. And so let us look at that first property and effect: purpose.

Real penance is always purposeful. And this characteristic is also an effect; that is, the more we truly realize our state as penitents, the more purpose we have to amend. We know that, in the Sacrament of Penance, we cannot be absolved from our sins if we do not have a firm purpose of amendment. Contrition is not real—it is not only incomplete, but it is not real—if there is no true purpose of amendment. This does not mean that we may not fall again, but it does mean that I am full of purpose, that I am not going to go on like this, that I am not going to keep doing this. That is what characterizes real penance. A weak wailing about my faults, with no evident purpose to do anything about them, has nothing to do with penance. It has a lot to do with cowardice, it has a lot to do with pride, and it is an expression of lack of purposefulness. But real penance is a driving force. We see this dramatically in our Father Saint Francis. He wept because "Love is not loved." He just could not get over this, and he was so driven by this, that Love was not loved enough by him. He went on with such purpose that in the sacred stigmata, love finally broke out all over him.

Real penitence can always be detected or its absence noted by purposefulness or the lack of it. Purposefulness shows the presence of penance: "I am really going to do something about all the wrong I have done, all the poor responses I have made, all my defects." That same purposefulness is an effect of penance; that is, the more penitent we are, the more purposeful we become; and the more purposeful we are, the deeper is our understanding of penance. It is the person of little purpose who doesn't see much need to do penance.

The second characteristic and effect of penance is, manifestly, alertness. A person who is penitent, who is growing into an understanding of her great sinfulness, her notable faultiness, is a person who is very alert for occasions to make reparation to God; whereas the person who is not aware in a purposeful way of her own defects and deficiencies inevitably has a very sharp eye for real or supposed deficiencies in others and is very unalert, that is, does not even recognize occasions for reparation. We miss the point so often. Our Lord is giving us an opportunity to make reparation in this act of humility for our many acts of pride; because we have been so often impatient, he is arranging this occasion for us to make reparation by patience; and so on. The person who has a sense of being a penitent, of needing to do penance, will be very alert for these. This alertness and this purposefulness are joined and conjoined.

We see this purposefulness in the tax collector Zacchaeus and in his determination to *do* something about penance. He didn't say: "I'm sorry. I was a victim of circumstance and all my forebears have lived like this. And some of them did worse than I did, and let me tell you what some of these others did." Instead he became a real penitent, a man of purpose. He was going to pay back everything, and pay it back fourfold. He was so alert to see how he could do this.

Zacchaeus is also an outstanding model of the third characteristic of true penance, which is joy. Up there in his tree, Zacchaeus fully saw what a rotter he had been. He had no taste at all for saying what other people were doing; but he saw what *he* did; he became this man of purpose, and he became so alert to opportunities for reparation that he said he was going to pay back fourfold. And he was obviously joyous. You can see him scrambling down out of that tree and going off to lunch with Christ, very penitent and very joyful. The remembrance of our sins and our faults, if we have true penitence, never begets bitterness, never begets melancholy. It always begets purpose, alertness, and joy.

This is what is so deeply in my heart during these Advent days, which I want you to take deeply into your own heart, your own reflection, your own prayer. If we look at this in reverse: when we are not joyful, we can always know that we are not penitent. When we are not alert to make reparation for our sins and our faults, it is because we do not have any really prayerful awareness of them. We simply see a situation that calls for effort that I do not want to make; a situation that calls for generosity I am not prepared to give; a situation that calls for me to humble myself in a way that I do not wish. But the penitent sees something so different, and the penitent is joyful. You see the real penitent always ready to go, full of purpose, full of alertness, full of joy. Like Saint Francis, we are all called to be joyful penitents.

❖ ❖ ❖ ❖

Jubilant Rejection

AT THE little Chapter of Lauds today, Isaiah tells us that our dear Lord in his humanity learned to reject the bad and to choose the good. That thought is so intriguing— let us explore, as far as the limitations of our understanding will allow, the humanity of Christ and the things that any child learns by rejecting the bad and choosing the good.

A child learns by mistakes to reject what is not good, and to choose what is good. For instance, he learns that it is not good to put his hand on that hot stove. Of course, our Lord never had to learn what our fallen nature must learn—that is, to reject evils—but on the human plane he did have to learn to reject what was not good and to choose what was good. He did have to learn by suffering to reject temptation, for we are told clearly in the Scriptures that he was tempted. His public life began dramatically with temptation, and it ended with terrible temptations: the temptation to deep anguish of soul in the garden of Gethsemane, and the temptation on the Cross to think that he was forsaken by his Father. The public life began with temptations, but it did not quite end with temptations, for after that word of agony, "Why are you deserting me?" came the word of faith and complete trust: "Into your hands I commend my spirit." Humanly, he could say, "Even though you seem not to be present, I commend my life into your hands." There has never been a greater act of faith than that.

Rejection may seem a dismal or negative word; and in fact, in the way we often use it, it is indeed a dreadful word. We talk of people being rejected. There are many people in our society who are rejected: family members rejected by the family, persons rejected by the governments. However, rejection can be either horrendous or glorious, depending on what is rejected. Searching our souls with God's light in prayer, we want to see what we need to reject, and what we must not reject.

What does the word *reject* mean? It comes from Latin re- and *jacere*—literally, "to throw back". There are things that can be taken to our hearts only if we reject other things. "Rejection" becomes a glorious word when, enlightened by prayer and energized by practice, we "throw back" everything that keeps us from God and from living our lives as we are called to live them: in truth, in love. It is much like the Latin word *abnegare*. Abnegation is not much spoken of in our times. Our society tells us that there should be no abnegation, that all is positive; the workshops and the columnists all tell us there is never a need to exercise any abnegation. Yet abnegation is a *royal* word, for it implies an act of choice. I *choose* not to do this; I say "no". That is a royal act, and so too is the act of rejection, when we throw back the things that keep us from living the life to which we have been called, from achieving the height to which God summons us each day. Where do we throw these things? Into the trash pile, where we burn them up in truth.

Although each of us will readily see, through prayer, many things which should be rejected, I want to linger today on three particular things that we *must* reject. The first one is self-deception and manipulation of the truth. At first we might think, "We would never do that!" And yet we know how easily we can do it in little infidelities (if we may ever qualify infidelities with the adjective "little"). We might never deliberately not obey, not respond promptly and joyfully; but we might tell ourselves that it would be so good just to finish this, even though the bell has rung. Little dreary things such as this are manipulations of the truth. No one is malicious; no one says, "This is really wrong, but I don't care, I'll do it anyway." Rather, we manipulate. We deceive ourselves into believing that, for this good reason, I must do that; or that I can't rise to this because of that. Giving myself an excuse for a lack of charity, undoubtedly very soon I will fail to call it uncharitable at all. This is the way that self-delusion begins and can prosper in our lives: by our facing the truth less and less. We become more and more self-deceptive, manipulative, and deluded.

Our Lord tried many times in the Gospel to save people from self-deception, sometimes with gentle but piercing questions. For instance, he tried to save the apostles from their ambition and worldly squabblings when he asked, "What were you talking about on the way?" Later, when Peter said, "They will all deny you, but I never will", Jesus tried to save him from self-assurance, from the self-delusion that he would never fail, by looking at him with great love and saying, "Even before that cock crows twice, this is what you will do." He tried to save the apostles from thinking, "We want to be first! And that's a wonderful place to be—either to the right or the left of the Lord." They didn't face the truth that to be first is to be last, and to choose the last place is really to be first—as he had been teaching them all his life. In the end, Jesus did save the apostles from their petty ambition; and he did save Peter, making him the first pope. Greater than being the first pope was his humility and spirit of reparation. All the ancient legends say that Peter wept the rest of his life, and it is not hard to believe that. He didn't gloom; he went forward and worked and labored and was martyred. He allowed himself to be saved by God, and humility triumphed. And Peter not only governed the Church, but was crucified upside down, thinking himself unworthy to die in the same position as his Lord and Master.

Jesus tried to save the Pharisees from their terrible self-deception that they were "right", always upright, doing the right thing, never admitting they did a wrong thing. He tried to save them with terrible and excoriating terms: "You hypocrites!" "You lie!" The apostles hadn't lied when Jesus asked them what they had been talking about; they didn't say, "Oh, we were just talking about how we could be more humble." But the Pharisees went right on lying, and so he could not, so to speak, save them from their self-delusion.

In psychology we speak of the "pathological liar"—a person who no longer knows he is untruthful because he has deceived himself for so long. This does not mean he is not guilty; rather it means that guilt has reached its consummation. A line has been crossed. In our own lives, in the matter of our habitual infidelities, we can move toward that line in so-called "little" ways, terrifying as that may sound. When it becomes "all right" to cut this corner, to indulge myself in this little way, we move further and further away from the truth and closer and closer to that terrible line which is complete self-delusion, self-deception. Every day we must reject any least untruthfulness to ourselves, such as, "It's all right to have this without permission because I really need it, and there is no need to ask because I'm sure my superiors would want me to have it." Or, "There's really no need to be prompt because I truly have to finish this for a very good intention." Or, "There's no need to give myself fully to the work and the labor because I really must spare myself, as I want to serve for a long time." This whole company of delusions leads us further and further from the truth. We no longer recognize the truth when we indulge in these little untruthfulnesses, upon which fall the most terrible judgments of God. "Maybe I was impatient, but it was because of that; maybe I was irritable, but look at what provoked it."

It is such a help if we remember that Isaiah says, "No single thing escapes him." Christian families often used to have (and some monasteries still have) a sign saying, "God sees me", or sometimes simply a picture of an eye. Although we might consider it self-evident that God sees me, still we can sometimes act as though God did not see me, as though God did not know what I am thinking or doing, as though God did not know my motives or my subterfuges. God sees me; no single thing escapes him.

A second thing we must reject is the demand to know. Since there is a certain good root in the desire for knowledge, we might not have given it too much thought as a thing to be rejected. Even on the secular plane, we want to know things and we like the fullness of truth. One who does not want to know will never be a true scholar or even a true student. However, in the spiritual life, we do great damage to faith and to hope by demanding to know how things will turn out—by demanding, "What does it mean? What is the hour? What is the day?" Our Lord corrects this fault again and again in the Gospel, where we find the apostles continually saying, "Show us!

We want to see! We want to know!" One really remarkable statement in the Gospel is, "Show us the Father and that is enough." And our Lord replies, "No one sees the Father but I. Have I been with you so long a time, and still you are asking questions like this?" The apostles ask again and again, "When will the kingdom come? When will you establish the kingdom? Will you do that now?" Our Lord never answers.

There are also all the questions about when the world will end, which he does answer: "It is not given to you to know, but only to my Father." If we are really to live a life of faith and of hope, we must reject that demand to know, although it is a very searching demand. However, upon examination of it through prayer and pondering, we realize that if we knew the whole, our opportunities for faith and for hope, both of which are the witness of things not seen, would be taken from us. We would have no opportunity either for faith or for hope if our Lord were to say to us, "Here is a thing which you must suffer now, but by nine o'clock tomorrow it will all be cleared up, you will see my purpose in this, and everything will be just great."

Remember how Saint Paul wanted to be delivered of that mysterious sting or temptation—I doubt he would have been satisfied if our Lord had said, "It will be only for six months and then you will feel wonderful again", or, "It's all going to be over next week, and I will show you then what I mean by all this." Instead, he gave Paul that mysterious and wonderful word: "My grace is sufficient for you." Sometimes it's very hard for us to accept this, because it doesn't seem sufficient. We squirm and suffer and everything in us demands that this thing be resolved. But God is saying, "My grace is sufficient for you; it is not yours to know the day or the hour."

The rejection of the demand to know is not like the first rejection, that of self-deception, which as the worst kind of trash must be thrown back on the trash heap where it belongs; rather, the demand to know should be tossed back into the bosom of God as a gift. The burning demand to know, to have all resolved, to have everything figured out, to have everything clear, to know the reason why God permitted this, to know the answer to that ageless cry of man: "Why is there evil? Why is there pain?"—we give it all as a gift, we toss it back with all reverence to God, who (and I say it with even more reverence) catches it with delight.

The third thing we must reject is perhaps the most piercing of all: the temptation to say, "What's the use?" In our battles waged (sometimes not very energetically) against our faults and our failings, we can see the evil within us, but we say to ourselves, "I put as much energy as I have into this battle and nothing seems to be working out well." Sometimes we are able, with our limited understanding, to say honestly, "I really have tried my best, and things haven't turned out well, have not reached a happy consummation." Do we not all experience this temptation to say, "Oh, what's the use?" with all our faults, especially those which we have been trying to overcome for years and which are still there? To say, "Oh, what's the use?" is, of course, to give oneself an excuse not to do it. The next step is to stop trying; to give up.

When our Lord, in the garden of Gethsemane, saw with his humanly enlightened intellect and the perfect light of his divinity that some were not going to profit unto salvation by what he was about to undergo, he really sweat blood; and that terrible cry, "Take this chalice away from me", was the temptation of "What's the use?" This same temptation must have beset him on a lesser scale earlier (although one hesitates to classify any of Jesus' sufferings as "lesser"—but not on the complete scale of Gethsemane) when the lepers whom he had healed didn't bother to come back to thank him. Jesus showed how hurt he was by people who did not bother to make a return, a response, and in that he expressed the human temptation he felt of, "What's the use of working miracles? There are nine out of ten who don't even bother to thank me."

Reading the Gospel with care, we can see the same in many other instances in his life. Certainly he had this temptation with his little community of apostles; for although he kept teaching them, still they never seemed to learn. However, he always rejects that temptation (and one says this very carefully because we must tread with care and humility in this mysterious area of the humanity of a Divine Person); and out of the rejection of this temptation again and again, he gathered the human strength to say after "Please take this chalice away", his "Whatever you will—thy will be done."

Let these not be dismal ponderings, but rather part of our determination. Let us be fully alive, and ask ourselves, "What am I doing with my life?" It is the only life I have, and I am determining my eternal life by the way I live my earthly life. What are the things that cannot enter into eternity? Anything that is not the truth; anything that is not love. May we begin a pattern of jubilant rejection of the things that take us from the way, which lead us apart from the truth, and leave us not fully alive.

✥ ✥ ✥ ✥

Thursday of the Third Week of Advent

Success

My dear sisters, when we were singing Psalm 118 recently, I was so struck by one of its verses, at first glance mysterious, then revealed after pondering as deeply theological: "O Lord, grant us salvation; O Lord, grant success." The psalm is telling us in that line that salvation is the only success there is, and it is given. And so we pray for it. We pray that we will be successful in allowing God to save us all the way. Now I think this very readily relates to that great figure of Advent, Saint John the Baptist, that saint about whom we know a great deal; in fact, there are very few persons about whom we know so much before the person is even born. We know quite a bit about his parents, we know what made him dance around before birth, we know about his unborn reaction to the presence of Jesus. Then we know quite a bit about how he lived his very penitential, prayerful life and how he minced no words with those who flocked to hear him. He was never the person of the soft word—always the kind word, yes, but often this kind word was very, very firm as when he told them, "Repent, right now. The time is at hand." When they asked him questions about what they should do, he gave them very forthright answers. And then, we know he went on to imprisonment and to what eventually led to his death, a most ignominious death: the wages of a woman's lust, of a king's lust before a cheap dancing girl. What a death for the man of whom Jesus had said, "There is no man born of woman greater than John the

Baptist." And so there is very much for John the Baptist to teach us; and perhaps the greatest thing he teaches us is his saying "He must increase; I must decrease" (Jn 3:30).

We talk very much in our time about the theology of Father So-and-So, and the theology of Doctor So-and-So, and the theology of Professor So-and-So; well, this is the theology of John the Baptist and it's one sentence. It didn't take a book; it took only one sentence: "He must increase; I must decrease." Relating this to Psalm 118, I must be similarly successful. I must allow myself to be saved. We see that the whole thrust of our vows is that I should decrease and God should increase. That's really their purpose. We don't make a vow of obedience because we want other people to tell us what to do, or because we have no idea what to do with our will and so we'd better submit it; we have no ideas of our own, anyhow! All of our vows are made just so that God may possess us, that he may have all the room. And we know, dearest sisters, in our more lucid moments, that if we are not busy at letting him increase and making ourselves decrease, we find that we take up more and more room within ourselves so that there is less and less room for God.

Saint John tells us that Jesus "must increase" and, in order that this should be, "I must decrease." Our aim is not that I should decrease until there's nothing left of me: here I am, an empty shell! That's not the purpose of it. We all learned in physics that nature abhors a vacuum. Probably you performed the same scientific experiment that made us all feel very learned when we were sophomores in high school, of creating a vacuum so that you could hear the air rush into it. And the air would really screech into that created vacuum. I found this very thrilling. I'd do this again and again to hear it. And so even nature does not want anything empty, nature does abhor a vacuum, nature comes in. A thousand million more times spiritually, dear sisters, does God come into a created emptiness of ourselves. God truly rushes in, more than the air rushed in during those youthful scientific experiments. He does rush in with his grace, with a spiritual sound of rushing wind as was heard at that first Pentecost. He does not want us to be empty, to leave us empty. He wants us to decrease so that he can get in. What he wants most of all is that he can be totally there, so that we are all his, and all the space is his.

Each vow is calling us to decrease so that he may increase, and is giving us the power to do that. Every actuation of our vow of obedience is admitting the obedient Christ more into that emptying out of my wayward, willful self. He became obedient. How long? Unto death. How much unto death, in what way unto death? Completely, totally. So, every act of obedience is letting the obedient Christ increase in us. And then, when the obedient Christ is in charge in his domain, then we begin to experience the marvel of the paradox that, when he is completely there, then the more I am really myself. When I decrease, that God may increase, he brings me to myself in a way that I was not there before. For, as Saint Paul tells us, "You are in Christ."

With our vow of chaste love, every expression of love of God, of love of sisters, lets God increase in us because he is love. And this is accomplished by our casting out of ourselves all the unloving things, the little indulgences of our moods, the little rehearsing of real or imagined hurts, the little stirrings up of small inward hostilities, the little resentments in which Christ can have no part. He can't be there. He is love; and in so far as love has possessed us, he is there. And insofar as it is not there, as we are full of small unloving things, unloving words, unloving glances, unloving acts, he is not present. Our unloving self is increasing all the time, whereas he should be increasing, he who is love. This is the purpose of the vow of chastity, and I repeat it: it is the power of the vow to let him in, to let him increase.

With our vow of poverty, made to live "without anything of our own", it is a wonderfully helpful examen to take stock of what we do claim for our own. Now I am sure there is no one in community who would like to claim for her own a couple of easy chairs for her cell or a Beautyrest mattress or a wardrobe of varied clothing. It makes us laugh to say these things, but there are more insidious things to have for our own, sometimes frightening things. We touched on this in the vow of chastity, but it relates very much here. Is there any little resentment that is my own? Is there some little hurt that is my own and that I think about a lot? Do you know we can claim a neurosis as our own? And we don't want to give it up! I foster this little neurosis and I take care of it; it's my own. We should really confront ourselves with these things. Do I realize that these things gather a terrible interest? A neurosis can become a psychosis as it gathers interest upon itself. A resentment can become a hatred. A nurtured hurt can become a moldering thing that leads to a real psychotic depression. These things sound frightening; and that's good—I want them to be. Let us all love to examine ourselves this way, from time to time. We love the ring of the phrase "without *anything* of my own". What do I most tend to keep for my own? It's amazing what we will discover, sometimes, if we are honest. We really wouldn't want to keep spiders in the cupboards of the house. We wouldn't want to keep spoiling food in the ice box, and to watch it and see if it's there and if it's gathering more bacteria. But we can do this spiritually, keep these things for my own. This is my hurt, and it's getting moldier all the time. Yes, it's healthy to laugh at these things, because then they are already in a certain sense defeated. When we laugh at wanting to keep a hurt, we are already in some sense no longer doing it. So, we let the poor Christ increase in us by a decrease of these things that we keep for ourselves.

Then, our vow of enclosure unites us to the praying Christ, always united with his Father. Every time that we foster prayer, that each in her own way tries to grow in that spirit of ejaculatory prayer so essential in our life, every time that I strive to foster recollection, I am letting the praying Christ increase in me, and letting myself and all my "rattle-bang" of thoughts decrease. We want the noise to die out and the prayerful Christ to come in.

And so, in the little things of every day, let us love to seek out the ways in which he can increase and I decrease. Every time that I smile at a sister, when I feel like frowning or showing that I'm displeased or have been intruded upon or don't feel understood, Christ is increasing in me. Every time that I humble myself, the meek and humble Christ is increasing in me and my proud self is decreasing. We should not be so foolish as to waste these opportunities. How many occasions of grace we can waste, while our blessed Lord wants so much to increase in us! He wants to rush in, more than air ever wanted to rush into that created vacuum. He *wants* to do this. And so, let us let him in. Let us allow him to increase; we do this by calling ourselves to decrease. Who wants to be full of self?

When we see a person who is obviously full of herself, it is not an engaging picture. It is very disaffecting to see a person full of self. But to see a person full of Christ (and it is unmistakable when this is genuine), oh, how engaging *that* is! How inspiring that is. How ennobling that is. So, let us return to the point of beginning: "O Lord, grant us salvation; O Lord, grant success." May we come to realize, as Saint John realized and invited others to realize, that this is the only success there is: to let Jesus triumph in us, to let him possess this little field that I am. This is success. Our world now is nearly mad with its own idea of success. Success is to get ahead in the business world, to possess a lot of things, to have a lot of everything. Success is to be a famous name. And that is the very reason why salvation is often forgotten: because this blindness prevents us from understanding what the psalmist knows, that salvation—allowing ourselves to be completely saved, completely one with God, completely possessed by God—is the only success. Let us be intent on being *very* successful contemplative women.

✣ ✣ ✣ ✣

FRIDAY OF THE THIRD WEEK OF ADVENT

High Ambition

Observe what is right, do what is just (Is 56:1).

THIS MORNING the first reading at Mass brought to my mind a line from the New Testament: "Have no ambition except to do good" (Tit 2:14). We want to reflect together on that idea of ambition. We don't have to sit down and hold our heads and rack our brains and study up on what is good, what pleases God. We already know so well. We know that love pleases God, because he is love. Every act of love of him, every loving look, every loving word, and every loving deed toward others pleases God. And this is the good we can do, all the time.

We know also that humility pleases God, for he has told us so. There are opportunities for this every day. We know that mercy pleases God, who is all-merciful. We know that in our intense way of life there are many opportunities for merciful understanding every day, and that by them we can please God. We know that prayer pleases God, and that we can make our whole life a rhythm of prayer. We really can do this. When the Apostle says, "Pray always, without ceasing", he would not ask us to do something that is not possible. We can foster in ourselves a rhythm of prayer in such simple ways, with nothing driving about it. We don't need to be "vocalizing" all the time. We can have little whispered conferences with our Jesus as we walk down a hall; we can say his Name as we come down each step. It is really not that hard to pray all the time, but we often forget this and instead waste the time in distraction, in thoughts that are better forgotten, in considerations that do not deserve our attention. Let us be mindful of this and see if we cannot establish a much deeper rhythm of prayer within ourselves.

We know that the sacrifice of obedience also pleases God. He has said that obedience is more pleasing to him than all the holocausts spread out in such imposing array in the Old Testament: "Obedience is better than sacrifice, and submission than the fat of rams" (1 Sam 15:22b). And we can do this! We can obey all the time and live in the presence of *Deus observans* always.

"My Hurt Beloved"° speaks of still other ambitions to please him: "Thee will I walk, unshod and smitten. Thee will I tell, and who will listen? Thee will I live in high ambition." And why do we aspire to this? It is "to ease thy hurt, Beloved". If this is our high ambition, we can achieve that.

We want to ask ourselves a few more questions about our ambitions to please God. Am I really living a spiritual life, or am I just performing spiritual exercises? Do I take a spiritual view regarding all these things that please him? What is the pattern of my life? It is not so much a matter of what my life *sometimes* is: whether it is sometimes a high peak of emotional fervor or sometimes a lassitude, a niggardliness about love and sacrifice. All of us make mistakes, and we depart from the right pattern. But, what is the usual, the regular *pattern* of my life? And what am I doing to make the right pattern more obvious to myself so that I see more quickly when I am getting away from the pattern, so that I can go back to it? This is a wonderful thing. Not that we never fail, that we never do wrong; for

° One of Mother Mary Francis' own poems.

this will never be—we are fallen, we are weak. But that we realize more quickly, more surely, more profoundly when the pattern is askew.

Then, what is the degree of my eagerness to do good? Is it a little eagerness, a "sometimes" eagerness? Or is it real eagerness of the will? I do not mean an emotional eagerness, but the eagerness of the will to do good for God, for his Church and for our sisters. What is the degree of my eagerness to do this?

Let us ask ourselves, also, how high are my ambitions? Are they not sometimes very, very dwarfed? I am ambitious to get my own way. I am ambitious to have my plans remain uninterrupted. I am ambitious that I should always be understood, though our dear Lord was not. We say, "I come to do thy will, O God." But is it sometimes my own will that I am coming to do (and coming pretty fast, and coming with a lot of force)? What are my ambitions to please him, and how high are they?

Then, after all of these questions, we must realize what remains: faith, hope, and love—and that none of these is spontaneous. Faith is a suffering thing. We cannot claim that because we believe, we therefore know and understand all things and how everything is going to turn out, and just what is its purpose; or, theologically, that we fathom all the mysteries of the Church, we understand exactly the Blessed Sacrament, we understand the Three Persons in one God. This can never be. Faith is a suffering thing: we do not know, but we believe. Sometimes, when sufferings come into our individual lives, into community life, we don't understand, but we believe. Hope is a suffering thing, because it reaches beyond what we can see, what seems likely. Neither faith nor hope is spontaneous.

Nor is love spontaneous. Now, we might hesitate a little bit and say, "Well, if you love someone, when you see that person a spontaneous surge of love rises up." Yes, that is, so to speak, an expression of love. But it is not love. Love is a thing of endurance, not just of emotional response; it is not a "sometimes" thing. Any love that is real has to be infused with suffering. Jesus' love for us was a very suffering love. In fact, love, if it is measurable at all, is measurable by how much it is willing to suffer. We have an indication of how much we love God by how much we are willing to suffer that God's will be done.

We can gauge, perhaps, how much we love the Church by how much we are willing to suffer for her, by how much we go forward to make reparation for every wrong done to her. That is the measure of love. How much are we ready to suffer for the Church, always putting her interests before our own small ones?

How do I know how much I love my sisters? By how much I am willing to suffer for them and, yes, from them, because this is the human condition, even in a united and loving community. If the redemptive love of Christ, which is the binding force of community, is present, then there has to be, even in the love, a suffering not only *for* but *from*—just as husband and wife must not only suffer for each other but sometimes from each other, because no one is perfectly understood.

Perhaps these seem somewhat scattered thoughts, but you will know how to weave them together. So, I wish for you now, I pray for you now, and I ask you to pray the same for me, peace and high ambition!

NOTE: Saturday of the Third Week of Advent: *There is no conference for this day because the Mass readings for the day will be those of December 17 or one of the following days for which there are proper readings.*

FOURTH WEEK OF ADVENT

❖ ❖ ❖ ❖

The Armor of Light

MY DEAR SISTERS, on this final Sunday of Advent, as on the previous ones, the Church is speaking to us, in the Little Chapter at Lauds, of putting off deeds of darkness and putting on the armor of light. Then, in Saint Matthew's Gospel, we have the appearance of the angel to Saint Joseph, calming his distress and bewilderment as to what he should do, and reassuring him. He describes this Child growing within the womb of the Virgin Mary, who is the fruit of the Holy Spirit and not of man. The angel, speaking to Joseph of this mysterious Child not begotten of man, describes him and his mission by saying: "He will come to save his people from their sins." The angel does not say, "Wait till you see the miracles he is going to work" (although he will do this: dead men shall come out from their tombs and the blind shall see). Neither does he speak of the Child's future suffering, his Passion, and his death. But he says, "He will come to save his people from their sins", as though this is his basic identification: Savior, Redeemer. This is a word of light, indeed, that the angel spoke.

Let us look together briefly at deeds of darkness and at this highly evocative and intriguing phrase, "the armor of light". Perhaps we are so used to hearing that poetic expression of the Scriptures that we may be tempted to rest in the poetry of it, but we must go on beyond the poetry. What does this mean? It is really a very strange expression. What has armor got to do with light? Isn't armor everything that light isn't and light everything that armor is not? Armor is so heavy; armor is a very strongly, heavily-made protection against attacks from without. The greater the battle, the heavier the armor. We remember the story of David. To help him in his battle with Goliath, Saul gave him armor that was so heavy that David couldn't move. That is the nature of armor: to be a very heavy protection against assaults from without.

What does this have to do with light? Why does God inspire the sacred writer to say "the armor of light"? When we ponder this in prayer it becomes very obvious that this armor is to protect from the attacks from *within*, not from without. It is the attacks from within that are really self-destructive. Attacks from without can destroy only the body. In the inspired word of Scripture our Lord says blithely, "Don't fear him who can destroy only the body." But fear destruction from within.

It is the armor of light, then, which is the protection against the destruction of the deeds of darkness from within. For where do the deeds of darkness come from? Not from outside, but from within. God made the world good. It is human beings who have made its evil dimensions, and all of these have come from the selfishness, the self-involvement, the consuming ambition of persons. What has destroyed nations? What has destroyed communities? The same thing that can destroy the person himself: deeds of darkness originating from within.

Light, we know, is a favorite word of the Scriptures, a favorite word of God. "I am the Light of the world", announces Christ. He is the light, first of all, of the little microcosm that is myself. His Mother we call Our Lady of Light, and in all of her appearances there has been this great element of light. At Fatima she appeared "clothed in light". She was wearing light, the little peasant children said. She had her armor very beautifully in place. At Lourdes there were rays of light coming from her. At Tepeyac the moon was simply something beneath her feet, because she herself was radiant with light. Light is a favorite theme of the Gospel. Saint John's great Prologue says he came as light into the darkness, and then adds that terrible phrase that there was darkness that would not receive him. This was darkness from within: darkness of the mind, darkness of the judgment, darkness of the emotions to which persons had yielded themselves up.

How do we check on whether these deeds of darkness are really destructive, are really "deeds"? Deeds, we know, begin in the mind. Deeds are the work of the will. How is it, then, that when we want to do good we find ourselves (as Saint Paul found himself before us) doing the opposite? These, I think, are not the deeds of the will, not the true deeds of darkness. These are the deeds of weakness. There is a ready and acceptable gauge on whether our faults, our sins, are really deeds of the mind and the will, or whether they are simply the effects of weakness. The Church herself talks about the "sin of surprise", which does not bear the same weight of guilt before God as the deliberate sin. There are the faults of surprise, too. How do we sort them out? What are the real deeds of darkness? Is this impatient or unkind word, this selfish deed, this self-involvement a real deed of darkness, or is this a deed of weakness?

In praying over this, it seemed to me that there are three clear effects that help us in our discernment, and these we must use to check on ourselves. I had to smile when I discovered that there is alliteration here: they all begin with "P". If it is a sin or a fault of surprise, there is the sadness of suffering in *peace*. That is the first "P". If we have spoken the impatient word, shown the irritability or annoyance, done an unkind thing or selfish deed, yielded to a pettiness, there is an almost immediate sadness and suffering, which, however, is not destructive of peace. There is peace *in* the sadness and the suffering; whereas turmoil indicates simply a thunder, a storm of pride that I did not turn in as good a performance as I want others to see me turning in.

And then, I think, there is *poverty*. There is no peace when we are not without excuse: "I was doing so well until somebody said thus and so, until somebody did this, until my plans were upset, until it didn't turn out the way I thought, until the time didn't work out, until I wasn't appreciated." But there is peace when there is poverty: "I am without excuse. I am not blaming this on anyone or any circumstance or any situation. I am very poor. I am at peace with this sadness, with this suffering, which I gladly bear as proper to what I have done, because this is not a deed of darkness of my mind or my will, but of weakness."

The third "P" is *purpose*. Peace and poverty and purpose: "I am going to make up for this today, fourfold. If I was unkind to one person, I am going to be fourfold kind to four others. If I have been impatient, I am going to be fourfold patient this day." There is a real purpose, which is related to the poverty and the peace. When we are in turmoil and not in peace because we are outraged at ourselves for having turned in a bad performance, then the others will not follow. We will immediately look for excuses: why I tripped, why I was standing on point but fell on my face, why I was going to make this beautiful pirouette and could not complete my turn and merely staggered around. Instead, we strive to be without excuse: "I didn't practice enough; I was trying to get beyond my limitations; my basic clumsiness showed; I need to work harder." And out of that comes the purpose.

We see in the first reading from Isaiah the cowardly Ahaz, who is covering up a real deed of darkness with right words that are not true, with artificiality. God says to him, "Ask for a sign from the Lord, your God." The words of Ahaz sound very good. These are not proud words. They are not impatient words, not self-pitying words. He said, "Oh, I would not tempt God." It sounds so humble, and it is so false. Sometimes what sounds like the right word is really an expression of the deeds of darkness, as with Ahaz. It could have been a magnificent word, if it were true; the trouble is that it wasn't. It was a cover-up. He did not want to face God. He did not want to face what the sign from God would demand of him. And so he says, "Oh, I would not tempt God. I would not ask for a sign." Let us remember that: he did not want to accept what the answer would demand of him. And so he has gone down in history as the cowardly Ahaz, as though this were part of his name—the artificial, the untrue.

It is the light, the armor of light, which protects us from these things. Wearing that armor of light against the deeds of darkness within sends our words, our glances, and our looks through a purifying filter of light. We have all seen pictures of knights in armor, wearing a visor to protect the eyes and a mouthpiece to protect the mouth from assaults from without. If the armor of light, the eye-visor of light, is really over our eyes, our eyes will be kind. Our eyes will look on our sisters as upon God, with love, very humble love. And if our lips are covered with the mouth protection of light, our words will be kind, they will be humble, they will be sweet, they will be quickly contrite.

Let us take deeply to heart these loved words of the

Church: "Cast off the deeds of darkness and put on the armor of light." Let this, then, be our great concern. Casting off the deeds of darkness and putting on the armor of light are not sequential acts; they are simultaneous. We cannot put off the deeds of darkness without putting on the armor of light. If we put on the armor of light, then already the deeds of darkness are cast out. The weakness, the feebleness, will pass through the armor of light and see itself wrong, showing this in the peace of sadness, the poverty of spirit, and the purpose.

✤ ✤ ✤ ✤

The Highly Favored One

WHAT DOES the Church tell us in her Good News, her selection from the Gospels for this final Sunday of Advent? We find again the account of the Annunciation. That alone would perhaps be conference enough. The Church cannot present this to us often enough. She shows herself in this so much a Mother, as she repeatedly sits all her children down and says, "Now this is how it happened. And this is what the angel said. And this is how our Lady responded. This is what happened afterward." A mother loves to tell small children, and small children love to hear, the same good story over and over again. It is so typical of children to have their favorite stories and to ask that they be told again. And this is the Church's favorite story. And so she tells us, again and again. Now, besides telling us the story, what is she saying to us about our behavior, about our manner of living, in this Gospel? What does it mean for us, besides the marvelous memory of what happened: the inspiration of our Lady's response; the marvel that one of our own, a woman with a body like ours, was chosen by God in a way that no one was ever chosen, or will be chosen. What of our *modus vivendi*? I believe if we take the words of the angel as spoken to *us* we will see it very clearly. There is so much in the four phrases of his message that each one would certainly provide a full conference, or several. But we will compress them into one, which you will develop in your own prayer.

What is the first word of the angel? "Rejoice." What does the word mean? I think perhaps we do not give enough consideration to the reiterative quality of the word. We know that when we say something should be renewed, we mean that it should be made new again. And when we say that something needs reforming, or was reformed, we mean that it needs to be formed again, or again be given its original form. The word *rejoice* means "be joyful again". And therefore, when Saint Paul says in his Epistle to the Philippians (taken by the Church on Gaudete Sunday, and really threaded all through the Advent liturgy), "Rejoice! And again I say to you, rejoice!" we could translate that quite literally by saying: Be joyful over and over again. And I say it to you once more, be joyful over and over again.

How do we put the "re-" into re-joicing? Is it not by being grateful for joy? Was this not characteristic of our Lady? The Scriptures tell us that she pondered things in her heart, which was her way of living—she pondered things. Certainly she pondered not only what was not clear to her, what remained to be unfolded (as we must ponder it), but she pondered her joy. Again and again she had joy, because she remembered and pondered. Each time we are grateful to God the joy is given again. God first gives the joy, and then he commissions us to give it to ourselves again and again. Does this not explain how people who live in what looks to us like utter misery are yet joyful, even those who suffer so much and sometimes are persecuted? They are always grateful for any joy God has given, and it is there again and again. What we want to have in joy is an active thanksgiving and not just a passive enjoyment. With all the joys and graces of Advent and Christmastide, we cannot be grateful only when God gives us some flash of understanding, when we see something that we did not see before, when we see where we are amiss where we did not see it before, when we see where we are at fault whereas before we were blind; but we must return to these graces again and again. We must not just have joy, but re-joice. Translated again quite literally, what the angel says is: "Be joyful again and again. Rejoice."

God says this to us not only in every joy that he sends, but also in every sacrifice he sends, because in it he is saying, "I have found you suitable for my purpose. I ask this sacrifice of you." Who could not have joy and re-joice to have God say this? It is God, surely, who put into the mouth of his sweet Mother, when she appeared on Tepeyac, her words to Saint Juan Diego: "See, I place my hope in you." It came to me with joy, how God says this to us when he asks of us something difficult or something suffering: "See how I place my hope in you. For all your protests that you are not the one, see how our Lady says, 'I place my hope in you. I place my trust in you.'" She learned this from God; for all things are learned from God. And all words spoken rightly are struck off the Divine Logos, the Word of the Father.

We want to re-joice in joy, in sacrifice, and then, thirdly, in everyday contentedness, which we can regard under the superscription of poverty. What is it to be poor? Is it to be indigent? Not particularly. Indigent persons are often not poor at all. Is it to be rich? Often rich persons are not poor at all. To be poor is to be content with whatever God sends. As Saint Paul has told us: I know how to have, and I know how to be without. This is poverty: contentedness. We want to release to one another and to the Church the beauty of everyday contentedness, not to let the beauty of this escape us. Let us savor it, re-savor it, rejoice in it, always be doing something to release it. By our manner of living let us show to one another the beauties of everyday contentedness because we need one another so that we do not miss them. There is so much that we cannot see it all; we need one another to help us see and rejoice. "Rejoice!" God says to us. Be joyful again and again.

Then the angel addresses our Lady as the "so highly favored one." We need carefully to remember that the Son of God was not yet incarnate in the womb of the Virgin—she was not yet the Mother of God; she had not yet said her "yes"—but already there is cause for rejoicing. Already she is the highly favored one. Why was she at that moment already highly favored? She was already so highly favored because she was a unique thought of God (oh, how unique!); and yet each of us is, too. She was created by God; she was chosen by God. Each of us can be addressed in that same way: "highly favored one"—thought of, created, baptized, called to bear Jesus in our hearts, called to bear him physically every day in Holy Communion, called to spouseship, and then called to something to which our Lady was not called, something unique to us: to be forgiven. Now, by her Immaculate Conception, our Lady had the marvelous privilege of having no need to be forgiven, and we rejoice in this. Yet, we rejoice, too, in our own privilege (unique to us) to be forgiven. This is to be highly favored. We know, on the human level, that it is always a high favor to be forgiven. And so we are happy to be forgiven! We have the privilege to be forgiven by God, and to know that God will never withhold forgiveness. God has never yet refused forgiveness to one who said, "I am sorry, I am contrite." We are so highly favored.

Then the angel says, "The Lord is with you." There again is the great mystery. She is not yet the Mother of God. The question has not yet been put; the invitation has not yet been given. He does not say, "If you consent to what the Father asks of you, the Lord *will be* with you." He says, "The Lord *is* with you." What a shiveringly happy thought this is, that the angel can say exactly that to us. Not only in that most precious time after Holy Communion, but so long as we do not drive him from our souls—for we are in sanctifying grace—the Lord is with us. We have to respond and to live as those with whom the Lord is present. We must look like we have been saved; we must look like those redeemed; we must look like those created, baptized, loved, forgiven. We must look, above all, like those with whom the Lord *is*. It should show. It must show.

What do we say of someone whose holiness is so manifest? We say one sees Christ in him. One is so aware of the presence of Christ. This was said again and again of Pius XII, of Paul VI, of Pope John Paul II, of so many of the holy popes. Why was this? All these different personalities—some reserved, some exuberant, some tender—always elicited the response that Christ was within them, and that they were making this manifest, each in his own way. "The Lord is with you." The Lord was with our Lady, then, before he became physically incarnated in her womb. And the angel can say to us, too, "The Lord is with you." And we must be with him actively. It is only in the measure that we are with him that we are with one another. This is what it means to be a united community. It is not just a matter of camaraderie. It is not a matter of growing in affection for these persons who are so affable (or generally so!). The real unity of community depends on how much each one is with the Lord; for in the measure that we are with the Lord, then we are with one another in this little place. The community in which each sister is trying to be with the Lord is a community safe from disaster.

To think of that reality—"The Lord is with me"—is to be without fear. When we are with the Lord and conscious that the Lord is with us in sanctifying grace and in a most incredible way in Holy Communion, we can be happily, joyfully open and agreed to whatever the hours of the day unfold.

Then, we remember the fourth word of the angel: "Blessed are you among women." With humility, with reverence, with awe, we must take the responsibility upon us that these words, too, are spoken to each of us. Each of us is the loved one of God. Each of us is the one who must live in such a way as to make it evident that she knows she is loved. A woman who knows she is loved can do anything. This is a woman's strength. If a woman feels unloved, she is weak. She can still do, but not in the way that she can if she knows she is loved. Nothing is too hard to a woman who knows she is loved. Well, *we are*. We must deepen our own knowledge of that. We are blessed because we have been called by God to spouseship with the Son of God, and this call has been ratified by the community. We are so loved. We are blessed among women.

Oh, to how many religious, dearest sisters, is that spouseship, that brideship, the lost treasure of our times? So many things are catastrophically overturned, spoiled, ruined, devastated because the treasure of brideship has been lost. We have people doing good things with social justice. But why do they look so unlovely? Why do they speak in such an unloving way, when they want to do good things? Because this is the lost treasure: their brideship. But we, thanks be to God, and no thanks to us, have been preserved somehow, through someone's prayer or through the ineffable goodness of God to us in our weakness; he has kept us out of that maelstrom. We know where the treasure is; we know in what field it is hidden. It is hidden in the field of his Heart. So the treasure is not lost; we are blessed among women.

When those familiar words of the Gospel are read to us, let us accept the responsibility of the truth that God also speaks them to us. He gives us a plan of living when he says, "Rejoice. Re-joice." Do not let the joy trail away. Do not let any joy be ephemeral. Rejoice. What have I given you a memory for, and what do you remember? Do you count your joys like gold? Do you pray over your joys like your treasure? Do you rejoice that you are found worthy of sacrifice, considered by God a suitable person for something difficult? Do you release the joy, the high beauty of the everyday, in the contentedness that you share and break like bread with your sisters? Rejoice! The Lord is with you. The more conscious you are of his presence, the more you will cling to him and go guided as he intended, open and agreed to what the hours of this afternoon unfold—and the hours of tomorrow, and the hours of Christmas Day, and the hours of every day. Open and agreed, not put upon, not constrained. Highly favored one, to whom all this is revealed, blessed are you among women. We must accept the truth of this in awed humility.

❖ ❖ ❖ ❖

Great Expectations

WE LOOK BACK on this Advent as we enter into its final week. Certainly all of us look with contrition for many responses poorly made, maybe some responses not made at all. But we go forward into its final week also with expectancy. It is that of which I wish to speak: expectation.

This is a season of urgency and most tender expectation. It is the season of the expectation of the Virgin, as it was often called in ancient times. We want to ask ourselves some questions about our own expectations. What do we expect of God? What do we expect of our sisters? What do we expect of ourselves?

Now, it seems to me that expectation has three elements. We could express these in two different ways, which really come out the same. We could say that expectation has a height and it has a width and it has a length. Or we could shift a little to another perspective and say with equal truth that expectation has its quality, its quantity, and its durability.

Looking at the first perspective, we could say, "How high are our expectations of God?" That may seem a very strange question. Of course we expect everything of God. Then we pause and say: Do we? Do we really have such high expectation of God that we really think he will keep his word? When he says to our Lady through the angel, "Nothing is impossible with God", do we really believe it? Or do we think, when we get sloughed down in dreariness or slowness of the heart or mind, that, although we would not express it that way, this or that seems to be a little beyond God? *This* really is impossible. *This* situation will never change. *This* attitude will never change. *This* condition will never change. —We are saying that what he said is not true, that some things are obviously impossible to him.

Our attitude, upon examination, might show us that our expectation of God is not so very high. Our Lady's expectation was unlimited. Her cousin, Elizabeth, cried out, "Blessed are you because you have believed." Or, another translation says, "because you have trusted." We tend, although again we would not be quite so crude as to phrase it that way in words, to think that we will believe God can do the impossible as soon as he shows us, but right now we don't have the evidence. Our Lady didn't have the evidence either. She really didn't have much evidence all of her life. We could pause there for many examples, but you could find them for yourself. Her expectation was so high of God: he will do whatever he said he will do. All power has been given to him in heaven and on earth. He said that nothing is impossible with him, nothing at all. She believed this. Her expectation went right up and pierced the heavens. Part of that piercing of the heavens was to draw the Son of God into her virginal womb. One is tempted to linger there. You will linger there.

Then, how wide are our expectations of God? Do we limit him to a certain area? Or are our expectations of his power and his love always pushing out the frontiers further and further? Do we believe that he can do and he will do more and more things if our expectation is real, high, and wide?

And then, what is the length of our expectation of God? Does this horizon keep receding as we go further and further? We see more and more as our expectation, our high expectation, our wide expectation of God, takes us further and further, as we see his mysterious will unfolding. All of us have seen that in our own lives sometimes. Everything was going such a strange way, such an untoward way, and God was working out something we could not even have dreamed of.

Or, if we look at it from the other perspective: What is the quality of our expectation of God? Sometimes it is rather poor. We think he is omnipotent, but he doesn't really quite seem equal to *this* situation. We examine the quantity of our expectation of God. Do we think he is equal to every occasion, to every circumstance, to every problem, to every sorrow? Or do we think: This one seems to be a bit too much for God; he really can't handle this; maybe those other things, but this is one too many. Often God is just waiting for us to fill our measure of expectation of him before he acts. He can hardly act when we do not believe. How can he act when we do not hope? How can he act when our expectations are so limited?

Let us also examine the durability of our expectations. Are we dogged in our expectations of God? Maybe it doesn't look too great at this point. We don't see any light at the end of this tunnel. But we go forward in our expectation. One can say that, humanly speaking, it seemed a good part of the time that everything was going wrong for our Lady. It wasn't turning out right at all. But her expectation had such durability that it didn't wear out; it truly was indefatigable. How often we are very *de*fatigable: we expect, we believe, we hope—for a while. But then we get tired. Our expectation lags. And, so to speak, we hold back God's arm.

Then, what are our expectations of our sisters? Do we sometimes expect a poor response, which will often elicit just that? We have what can be an extreme advantage in our intense cloistered living, that in some ways we know one another so well, although in other ways we do not know at all what happens in the secret chambers of each heart and the secret struggles of each spirit. That sensitiveness toward one another always goes out; it goes out in waves. Even though the words may be right when we ask something of a sister, if the attitude is wrong, the sister will somehow sense it. And when our expectation is: "There probably won't be a good response here"—there will be a bad response much of the time. A poor expectation most often elicits a poor response.

We marvel that God can have such high expectations of us when we have given so many poor responses. And yet God goes on expecting us to be holy. He goes on believing and, to use our human expression, hoping that the next response will be better. God never says, "I am finished with you." He is indefatigable in his expectations of us, when often enough we give him very little visible ground for doing so. But God always expects that this time there will be a good response; or if there is a bad one, there will be quicker contrition, quicker confession of the fault, of the sin.

Our expectations of one another must be indefatigably so high that they will elicit good responses at God's moment. If we believe in one another in some small fashion as God believes in us, all counterevidence to the contrary notwithstanding, good responses will come; never doubt it. But we give up so easily, forgetting what would happen to us if God gave up because he said: "Look. I've got this list of twenty, thirty, forty, fifty, sixty, seventy years of poor responses." But God doesn't. God's expectation goes on, indefatigable.

And then we ask: What do we expect of ourselves? Sometimes we do not ask nearly enough of ourselves. And while we would be offended if we felt others would say, "Well, you can't expect much of her", we don't seem to be that offended that we expect very little of ourselves. We should confront ourselves about that. Do we really have a high expectation that, yes, I will overcome this sloth and I will respond? I will not yield to this murky mood, but I will respond. Is my expectation very low? "I can't do that; that's too much. That is beyond me." We don't expect ourselves to respond as a holy Poor Clare should, as a humble Poor Clare should, as a loving Poor Clare should. If our expectations of ourselves are so low, then of course we will gather a whole troop and army of excuses for ourselves. I don't need to expatiate on that dreary area; we all know about it.

These three are so interlocked. The more our expectations of God's omnipotence and God's enduring love falter, and if it looks impossible that this situation could be resolved or this person could change or this could happen, then, of course, our expectations of others will go right down with that; and our expectations of ourselves will go down into the level of multiple excuses. The happy converse of that truth is this: the more we do believe, the more we allow God to say, not only of his holy Virgin Mother but of us, "Blessed are you because you have believed", then, with that kind of expectation of God, our expectation of others rises and allows them to respond to our high expectations. With that comes a much higher demand on ourselves, a much higher expectation that we will not agree to be a mediocre person, a proud person, a complaining person, a person full of excuses, but a holy, humble, loving Christian.

The Sunday liturgy talks about high expectations. The prophet Micah in the first reading gives us the familiar passage about Bethlehem. Nobody expected anything much to happen in Bethlehem or anything great to come out of Bethlehem. The prophet says, "You [are] too small to be among the clans of Judah." You weren't worth mentioning. You are not only not the outstanding one, but: "Bethlehem, where's that?" Then he says, "From you shall come forth for me one who is to be ruler in Israel . . . [whose] greatness shall reach to the ends of the earth." What an expectation! He is talking about what can come from us if our expectations are high—if we could pray to God, "You have said nothing is impossible with you. I could be a wonderful exposition of this. If I respond, you could make a saint of me: a holy, humble, loving follower of Christ. How wonderfully your word would be verified."

In the second reading from Hebrews, the sacred writer says that God does not ask great sacrifices and offerings, and then adds, "I come to do your will, O God." This is what we can do. The Messiah said this is what he came for: to do God's will. This is heady wine. We can do the same thing he did. We can do God's will. That is all he said he came to do. We can do it. What about this for expectation? We can live as God's Son lived, if this is all we want to do: "I come to do your will, O God"—on this day which may drain me, this day which may surprise me, this day which may weary me, this day which may disappoint me. I come to do your will. We can live as he lived.

In the Gospel from Luke, we have a very small person become a prophet; an invisible person: little John, dancing for joy in the womb of his mother, expressing the great expectation that this other unseen person has come to redeem the world. His mother cried out, "Blessed are you who believed what was spoken to you by the Lord would be fulfilled." As the mother prophesied, so the very small prophet prophesied. But he prophesied with such high expectancy of what was to come that it was very noticeable to his mother, so much so that in this pre-Messianic setting of mystic expression from both, she stops to remark, "The infant in my womb leaped for joy." High expectation. As the Angel Gabriel had said, "Nothing will be impossible for God."

So, let us be occupied with expectation, and let us ask ourselves these questions over and over: How high, how wide, and how long are my expectations of God, of my sisters, and of myself? What are the quality, the quantity, and the durability of my expectation of God, of my sisters, of myself? *Great Expectations* is the title, we know, of one of Charles Dickens' great works. But it is the title of a greater work than Dickens, or anyone, could ever write. It is really the title of our Lady's life; and it is the title of every saint's life. Who are the saints? They are those whose expectations were the highest, the widest, the longest; of supreme quality, of multitudinous quantity, and of indefatigable durability. Peace and great expectations.

❖ ❖ ❖ ❖

Waiting

WE HAVE COME now to the final lap of our journey to Bethlehem, and surely a great sense of purpose and anticipation rises within us. What I would like to reflect on is that which is so radical to Advent: waiting. First of all, waiting must have a sense of focus. We know the parable of the wise and foolish virgins. The foolish virgins waited without focus on the right person, and so they waited languidly. The others waited with focus on the Bridegroom, and this gave them readiness. The ones who slept, not caring to think about the fact of needing oil in their lamps when the Bridegroom finally came, were very obviously focused on themselves. They were languid; they were tired; they went to sleep. Their own need was immediate to them; it was their primary concern. And so, they waited languidly, attending to their own needs, not thinking of his needs and the way to meet him; whereas the wise virgins were focused on him who was to come. They could not sleep and take their rest (which was part of this long waiting), unless all was ready for him.

The way our dear Lord deals with the foolish virgins in this Gospel parable is truly frightening. Maybe we would not think their conduct was all that bad—after all, they were tired; and later on they would be better able to prepare and to think about things with the proper focus on the Bridegroom. But what does he say to them? He does not say what we might have expected: "Now, why did you do that? Why weren't you foresightful? Why did you just give in to your own self-focusedness?" Instead, he says some truly chilling words: "*Nescio vos.*" "I don't know you. I do not know who you are." They knocked at the door and couldn't be admitted, because they were strangers to him. So there must be a focus in our Advent, and we know upon whom it is. All that we do in Advent is meant to focus on him who is to come. All that we do in life (of which Advent is a microcosm) must be focused on waiting for him who is to come.

We want to think about the focus of the young child, which leads us into the second property of waiting: action and service. The child says, "I can't wait for Christmas! I can't wait for my birthday!" What is a child doing when he says this? He is jumping from foot to foot. He is racing about. He is doing things. He's asking for things. He's getting things ready. I think what the child especially expresses so well is the deliciousness of waiting. When the child says, "I can't wait for Christmas", what the child so evidently means by his manner of behavior is: "I can hardly bear the joy of waiting. It's so great that I can hardly contain it."

Now, this same expression is perverted when we will not wait upon God's plan, or upon the needs of others. To use a personal example: Recently my sister and her husband narrowly escaped death. Their car was struck and demolished by another driver. Why was this? Because the other driver could not wait for the light to change. She went right through the red light because she couldn't wait. She had missed the whole purpose of the red light, which was that there had to be waiting so that there could be service to others, and so that all could go forward, in order, and in the discipline of charity to others. She got a dark reward indeed, nearly causing the death of two persons and injuring herself very grievously, because she did not understand about waiting.

God gives us red lights in our own lives, too. There is a difference between saying, "I can't wait! I can hardly wait for the light to turn green so that I can go forward; and meanwhile, I can hardly bear the deliciousness of waiting so that others may be served in charity," and saying the "Can't wait!" which just goes right through the red light. Unwilling to wait for something to be solved, unwilling to wait for the unfolding of God's plan, the wrong type of "I can't wait" goes forward, destructive of itself and of others. These are the two entirely different meanings of saying, "I can't wait." The latter is destructive, dark, and lacking understanding of the essence or the properties of waiting; while the former shows the knowledge and wisdom of the child who says, twirling around in an ecstasy of joy, "I can't wait! I can't wait!" Holy Father Francis knew this kind of waiting very well. As he waited for Christmas, he built a Christmas scene on Greccio. He could hardly wait for it to happen, so he wanted to see how it all was. He waited exuberantly. He waited joyously all of his life; and we see how he waited in suffering. We know that he waited upon his sons to grow in holiness. He didn't say, "I told you to do this! I gave you this counsel!" and do the equivalent of stomping his sandaled foot to show that he wanted results right now. No, he waited upon their growth. He waited upon the understanding of others without acrimony.

How did holy Mother Clare wait? She was full of action, full of service. She waited all her life for the approval of our Holy Rule, but she did not wait passively. She did not sit back and say, "If it will be, it will be." In utter trust upon God, she waited while asking again and again, but waited in activity, waited in service. This, too, is part of our Advent. We do not sit back and wait for Christmas. Our Advent is full of the activity of the child, full of the activity of our seraphic parents, full of petitioning: Thy kingdom come! Let Jesus' birth in me come to the Church and the world!

There is an expression which we are all familiar with: "waiting on people hand and foot". For instance, we will say of a very devoted son, when his aged and infirm parent dies, "Oh, he is such a devoted son. He waited on his father hand and foot." The waiting was full of doing. But this same expression can be said in a dark way, which can arise either from the unwillingness of the waiter or the unreceptivity of the one waited upon. We hear it said sharply, self-pityingly, or accusingly, "Am I supposed to wait on them hand and foot?" Yes, of course! And the waiting must be full of focus, service, and joy. Again, if the focus is wrong, if it's on myself and I'm thinking, "I'm expected to do more all the time! I have to do so much, and there isn't any gratitude, and my efforts are not understood", then this isn't real waiting. Real waiting is always focused on the other: on God, on the other person, on the Church, on the community.

There is another very ordinary expression that I wonder how often we ponder: someone has a job to "wait on tables". What do we mean by that? Not that you stand there and do nothing—quite the opposite! You are moving all the time. You are taking care of people's needs. You are watching out for needs; you don't even wait until they are expressed. You see that everyone is taken care of, that no one is missed. This is what we mean by waiting. And our dear Lord tells us that he rewards waiting—with waiting! Isn't that marvelous? "Blessed are those servants whom the master finds vigilant on his arrival. Amen, I say to you, he will gird himself, have them recline at table, and proceed to wait on them" (Lk 12:37). The reward for focus, for service, for active waiting upon the Lord is that *he* will wait upon *us*. I think that is the most marvelous truth that the Church shows us in the Scriptures. This is how he rewards us for right, energetic, focused, joyous waiting for him. God always does this. When we wait upon him, then he waits upon our needs.

Who would not want to wait upon Jesus hand and foot? Well, so often the answer is that *we* are the ones who do not want to do this. Where is he? In the tabernacle, yes; in the word of Scripture, yes; and in the persons in this room. We want to wait upon him hand and foot in one another, so that he may wait upon us. The more we do this, the more do we enter into the joy of the child, who says in the right way, with the wisdom peculiar to the child, unencumbered by the complexities and rationalizations of the adult, "I can't wait! I can hardly bear the deliciousness of this activity of waiting!"

How do you wait for someone whom you really love? You do all kinds of things; you have all kinds of surprises awaiting the loved one. It is an expression of love. Real waiting always begets this loving "doing". It eases the burden of waiting, which otherwise can scarcely be borne, as the child knows so well. The person waiting at the window is full of activity. When we are waiting for the loved one to come down the road, our heart is pounding, our eyes are straining, our whole body is taut, leaning forward. Someone is coming! Someone whom we love is coming! And now, in Advent, the One whom we love above all is coming. The Church is giving us these precious days to focus the eye, to let the heart pound because he is coming. He will come. By the love of waiting for his little red lights that say, "Step back, now, because someone else needs to be served", we will enter into the deliciousness of the real "Can't wait". We shall understand that when waiting is rightly comprehended, it is a deliciousness that is already indeed a wink of bliss.

May we spend these days waiting hand and foot upon Jesus, not only upon everything that he asks, but also upon all those needs that he hasn't expressed. Let us look for his needs, not even waiting until they are presented to us. The loving heart is always alert. It does not have to be told. Our sisters also have spiritual needs, which we must be alert to wait upon: the need for patience, for compassion, perhaps for forgiveness, perhaps for mercy, for understanding in a certain situation. The more we wait upon one another, the more profound will be our prayer. Waiting, rightly understood, is the depth of prayer and the measure of love.

❖ ❖ ❖ ❖

Lift Up Your Heads and See

Lift up your heads and see . . .
—Verse and response at Matins

MY DEAR SISTERS, the liturgy tells us: "Lift up your heads." And why? "Your redemption is at hand." Your redemption is right here. It is only days away. This text accents the acceleration of the liturgy as the days take us on so swiftly toward the birth into time of God. The celebration of this "is at hand." Lift up your heads and see.

I think there is another meaning here, too, which we must not neglect: that in the grace of each day, of each situation, God is saying to us, "Lift up your head. Your redemption is at hand." I think that if we would ensconce our thinking in this, we would often respond much better. It is the truth. Every opportunity to grow in grace is to be more fully redeemed. He gives us the occasions, especially in four accessible areas that we will consider.

What is redemption? We know that its basic, theological meaning is "rescue". It is an act of saving. Each time we are given a grace to change, to amend, God is reaching out his hand to rescue us from something that impedes this. We need to be rescued from the irritability that we can be so immersed in, with its inevitably accompanying ingratitude. We want to remember the terrible inverse ratio: the danger that the more we are given, the less we are grateful. And the other equally terrible expression of it—the exact equal ratio—is that the more we are given, the more we demand.

To rescue us from this danger, our dear Lord gives us occasions to overcome it. He provides special situations in which we must make an effort to be gentle, to be sweet and kind. He also gives the grace. This occasion is really saying to us, "Lift up your head. Your redemption is at hand." Rescue is right here; rescue from that irritability, those little and large angers of yours. Here it is! Lift up your head. It is at hand.

What is the result of that redemption? We have often considered the famous and chilling statement of Dostoevsky that many Christians do not look like they have been redeemed. When we are conscious of our need of redemption and when we allow ourselves to be rescued from these things that make us so much less than God desires us to be, we look happy. If we do not look happy it is because we are not letting ourselves be redeemed in all of these situations. We (all of us) have had many falls, but surely there have been times when we *have* responded: we wanted to be irritable; we wanted to be snappish; and we *did* realize that our redemption from this was "at hand". And, by God's grace, we *were* gentle and we *were* sweet and kind. What was the result? We were so happy. We have never yet had a person stomping around in irritability and anger who was just so happy. This has never happened. It is not only that the person does not make others happy, but also she is not happy herself. This is very evident. So, we can, and will, look redeemed when we do this.

A second, related example would be our impatience, to which we are all so subject. We want something, and we want it right now; we have this marvelous idea (and maybe it is), and we want the means to carry it out right now; we want all the time that is necessary to do it, and we want it right now—any of this familiar company. God is saying, "You need so much to learn how to wait and to perfect your very self-giving with this discipline. Lift up your head now. Your redemption is at hand, to be rescued from this impatience which in the end could devour you and spoil all your best desires." When we reach out and recognize that here is a chance to be redeemed from this impatience that wants to devour us, and if we receive and use that grace of redemption, what is the result? We are so much stronger. Impatient persons are very weak. A tide of impatience rises, and they go right down in the waters: glug, glug, glug. But when we choose to be patient, we are stronger. Strong persons are persons who can wait—sometimes wait in great suffering, wait in faith. But they can wait. The things that are selfish are eased out; the things that are really good are perfected, because they waited. And, again, we look redeemed.

A third example is that of pride. We know that pride blinds us. Our dear Redeemer says, "Lift up your head. Your redemption is at hand." Here is a chance to be humble, to humble yourself, to be sorry, to confess your fault, to leave off all the frills of excuses and to say you are really sorry, that you do not deserve to be forgiven but you would like to be and you ask to be—whether it is of God, or of a sister, or of community. The redemption of humility is being held out to this darkness of pride. What is the result? We are wise. Only the humble are wise; the proud are very stupid. Pride blinds us, and humility enlightens us. In humility we are wise; the light comes in. We remember our dear Lord saying in a moment of human exaltation, as well as of divine joy, "I give praise to you, Father, Lord of heaven and earth, for although you have hidden these things from the wise and the learned you have revealed them to the child-like" (Mt 11:25). Just as we are made happier when we accept redeeming from our irritability and our anger, as we are made stronger when we allow ourselves to be redeemed from our impatience, so we are wiser when we have allowed humility to redeem us, to rescue us from pride.

The fourth area in which we need redemption is superficiality, frivolity. The Spanish call it *frivolidad*. We can be rescued from this by a deep silence of thought, of mind, of heart, of word, and of action. God holds out these graces to say, "Be still", as he does say very directly in the Scriptures, "Be still and know that I am God." If we are living in a kind of froth of superficiality in the sense of not living our life deeply then it isn't only that, not being still, we do not know God, but that more and more we take on the place of God. I do this foolish thing and that foolish thing, because I have taken on the direction of my life; and it is not on the level of God. It is on this level of *frivolidad*. That word is used to apply to worldly things in a sense that I do not mean here. But we in our cloister can have our own *frivolidad*: our own seeking an easier, softer way, our own way of seeking our little and large conveniences, and so on. When God holds out this invitation to a silence of mind and of heart, and we accept it, what is the result of that? It is depth and control.

There will be multiple opportunities for this in these last precious days of Advent, in the little opportunities to be rescued from our irritability, from our impatience, from our pride, from our levity. Each one will be the coming King saying, "Lift up your head. Here! Your redemption is at hand." Here is the opportunity to be gentle so that you may be happier. Here is the opportunity to wait so that you may be stronger. Here is the opportunity to humble yourself so that you may be wise. Here is the opportunity to deepen yourself in silence so that you may know that I am God, and that the more I, God, am in control (*allowed* to be in control), so are you, at last, in control of your life, under *my* directions.

We *choose* to be redeemed. In our Lord's earthly life there were some who were with him every day, who heard his words spoken by his human tongue; there were those who saw his miracles; there were those who heard all his teaching; and they *chose* not to be redeemed. They chose not to be redeemed from their pride, their selfishness, their ambition, and their envy. It is a shuddering thought. Even after he was dead they were still trying to fix things, so intent were they on not being redeemed.

In our daily lives, in all the little (but really so large) opportunities, we don't want to choose not to be redeemed. We don't want to say to our Lord, "No, I don't ever want to be redeemed from my irritability, from my anger, from my pride, from my impatience. No, I don't want to be redeemed." Of course, we would say to this, "Oh, horrors!" And that is the right word for it. I think that if we present it to ourselves in this way we would be more aware of it. Day after day, situation after situation, we choose him; and we choose what is good for ourselves. We choose to be redeemed.

❖ ❖ ❖ ❖

DECEMBER 19

The Service of His Plan

MY DEAR SISTERS, it is with a sense of awe, certainly with a
sense of contrition, and hopefully with a great sense of
purpose, that we realize that less than one week from
today is the birth of Christ. And in this awe, this contrition, and this purposefulness we look as always to our
Lady. In the oration of the Fourth Sunday of Advent we
find the Church giving us the key to the whole mystery.
How did the Incarnation come about? Out of God's desire to redeem us. How did it all unfold? How do we go
about carrying forth his plan? The oration says that the
Word became flesh when the Virgin Mary placed her
life at the service of God's plan. Undoubtedly, we are all
moved at that particular oration set before us each year.
Within the mystery of the Annunciation, our Lady first
placed her life at the service of his plan. And, remember, it
was a plan she didn't understand. She asked one question
and that was all. It wasn't a very illuminating answer she
received. The angel said, "The Holy Spirit will come
upon you and the power of the Most High will over-
shadow you." Well, who is the Holy Spirit? The Holy
Spirit was to be revealed in the New Testament, which
was just beginning. We tend to think that this was a
great answer to her one question—and that this explained
everything. But it didn't explain much of anything, except
that God *had* a plan. And it was for her to agree whether
she would allow it to be carried out in her.

And then the angel's wonderful word, "Do not fear",

was a word which her own Divine Son was to repeat again and again: "Do not be afraid." Those who place their lives at the service of his plan never have any reason to be afraid. But when we place any of our energies at the service of our own plan, we have tremendous reason to be very much afraid. The most fearsome thing about it is that often we are not afraid at all. We want what we want, seek to carry out our own plans and to oblige God's plans to coincide with our own—and perhaps we are irritable and impatient and moody and morose because God is not in accord with our plan. And then, we should be very afraid.

So we want to remember that our Lady got an answer, yes—but it wasn't what we would call a very clear answer. In fact, one could say that, humanly speaking, it was more frightening than if the angel hadn't said anything. Who is this Most High? Who is this Holy Spirit? And what does this mean, that the Holy Spirit is going to conceive a Son in her? It was a very confusing answer, which did not lift the weight of faith from our Lady but made it more demanding. True, he gave her this sign about Elizabeth; and it is very touching that our Lady went off—indubitably to serve her cousin—but also to see the sign. Outside of that, she had a more demanding call to faith than before she had asked the question. And she accepted that, in not being afraid. She went forth and her reply to the angel was, "Be it done." We don't find our Lady saying in the most eloquent of ways, "This isn't at all clear what you're saying. I find it more confusing than before you spoke." Instead she says, "Be it done. And that I do not understand what you're saying does not take from me that grand possibility to say, 'Be it done.'"

Now, as I said at the beginning, we tend to think of

that as being the end of it, but this is only the beginning. Every day she placed her life at the service of his plan. It wasn't her plan at all that her Son would have no house to be born in. It wasn't her plan at all that they would get up in the middle of the night and ride off to Egypt in fear of his life—to a strange country where they knew no one, where they knew not the language nor the work of the people. Joseph was a carpenter and this was a land of stone masons. Joseph spoke Aramaic and they spoke Egyptian. All of this was a constant placing of her life at the service of his plans; and these really seemed, by human reckoning, very strange plans, certainly not plans that she could comprehend with her human intellect. But again and again she had to place her life at the service of his plan: Bethlehem, yes; Egypt, yes; back to Nazareth, yes.

Do we think of the little human "accompaniments" of those sparse Gospel revelations, that in Egypt they must have had just enough time to settle down and to begin to learn the language and for Joseph to set up a trade, perhaps to learn a new trade, before they had to go back? So, she placed her life at the service of his plan again. What was the strange plan when Jesus was lost in the temple? It wasn't her plan and she couldn't understand it as being part of his plan. Blessed words: "She did not understand". Back she went to Nazareth simply to be his Mother, to accept this strange word that she did not understand.

Even though she was acquainted with the Scriptures from her pondering and her prayer, and doubtless understood the Scriptures better than anyone else—being immaculate, her mind was unclouded and her heart uncluttered—she couldn't have grasped fully from the Old Testament, from the prophecies of Isaiah and the other prophets, all the terrible unfolding of the Passion.

Nor did she fully understand from any pondering or prayer the little daily passions that led to the bitter, blessed Passion—those daily passions of not being understood, of being unthanked, of being reviled, of being scorned, or of his continual disappointments even from his own. All of this she shared with him by continually placing her life at the service of his plan. And then there was that tremendous and climactic offering of her life to his plan in all the ignominies of the Passion, in watching churls mistreat her Divine Son. She had to accept this as God's plan.

We, too, are called to place our lives at the service of his plan every day. An example would be the community's general work, preparing the vegetables for each day's dinner. He has a plan there that we should work together in such love, in such gratitude that we have something to prepare and that there is work to do. He has a plan every day for the community's growing in sweetness and patience and humility at the general work. If each one is placing her life at the service of that plan, then the Word is being manifest. Perhaps that sounds like a very daring statement but you will understand how humbly I mean it. The oration says, "The Word took flesh on our earth when the Virgin Mary placed her life at the service of your [God's] plan." The Word is made known every time we place our lives at the service of his plan. Each one of us is a "word", an expression of God, in her own life. When we are really placing our life at the service of his plan at the general work, then, yes, by our manner of behavior there, by the sweetness that we bring, the patience, the humility, we could rightly say, "This is the Word of the Lord." These virtues are his "words", and he is made manifest by them.

Besides all of the tremendous and heart-rending

unfoldings of her life, our Lady had the little daily things that we have. I am very fond of picturing her waiting at the well, which she had to do every day with all the other village women. This was a kind of general work. We know what she brought to it—that as she waited her turn at the well she was no doubt helping the older or frailer women, placating those who might have been irritated by somebody taking too long, smoothing over the inevitable gossipy talk of some of the village women. She was again laying her life at the service of his plan. Things were always better where she was. Things were always sweeter and calmer at the well when she was standing in line.

Our Lady was always fulfilling God's ambition, and also her own ambition for herself. She called herself the "handmaiden": the lowest of the servants. She was very ambitious to be the least. Perhaps that is a large part of the reason that she is the cause of our joy, because humble people are always happy and proud people never are. She was the one who said, "Yes, I'll wait. I will not add another irritable word. I will bring the loving, calming word. I will be the one who sees something extra to do, not wondering why somebody takes so long at her turn, but seeing if I can help her." She was no less placing her life at the service of the Divine plan when she waited her turn at the well, than at any other time. This is a very bold statement, but it's the truth and the truth is always bold.

Another example came to me in prayer of how we place our lives at the service of God's plan. We are called in the name of the Church to perform God's own work, the *Opus Dei*, and his plan is that this should be a worthy incense of prayer in which we are totally involved with all of our energy, with all of our attention, with all of our enthusiasm—which need not be and often cannot be enthusiasm of the emotions, but enthusiasm of the will. This is placing our life at the service of his plan. There is a sense in which all Scripture was revealed in our Lady. All of our Lord's teaching about love, about humility, about throwing your life away if you want to keep it, about lowering yourself if you would be exalted, was fulfilled in her. Doubtless she would have said to others, "Look at him." I wonder if perhaps we will find out in eternity how many times he said, "Look at her." Should he not be able to say of his followers, "Look at them. My Scripture, my Word, is being fulfilled in them." In the Divine Office, at the Holy Eucharist, I am a "word" of the Lord. How is it spoken? Is it spoken with intention, with devotedness, with focusedness, with energy, with enthusiasm? We should make the Word more clear, not only when we read it, but much more when we live it, when we perform it. Years ago a close friend of the poet Sister Madeleva was extremely kind in saying that certain poems she had read° "made the Word a little less unutterable". I have remembered that and treasured it, certainly not as a compliment but as a call—as something our lives should do. We should make the Word a little less unutterable, a little more recognizable by the way we live and serve and love.

The third example is recreation, because God's plan at our recreation is that the community will draw closer together, the community will grow in the ability to trust and to share, to respond, to serve one another's needs. We think of our Lady at Cana when she was at the high recreation of a wedding feast and the supply of wine ran out. She was seeing this particular need, and perhaps many more, to fill. She was responding all the time. She was seeing needs and responding—hers was a very active,

° By Mother M. Francis.

participating presence. The Gospel says, delightfully, that Jesus came along because he belonged to her: the Mother of Jesus was there, and then "oh, and Jesus, too, was invited." She was an active participant. She was giving joy, being present, seeing needs, and thus doing what *we* could do to free ourselves, to liberate ourselves from our own incarcerating needs.

God has a great plan also in what we call the unexpected. It isn't unexpected to God. He planned it from all eternity. There is no happenstance in life, certainly not in the spiritual life. So often we say, "Oh, I didn't expect that to happen!" Well, God did. We could think, "Oh, that is what caused everything to go wrong", but actually that is what is supposed to make everything go right. There is nothing unexpected in all of creation. There is a plan in what we would call the unexpected. Wasn't the Incarnation the most unpredictable thing that could ever have happened? God has his whole master plan for each of our lives, for the community, for our holy Order, for the Church, and we should delight to remember that nothing should ever take us by surprise, except the wonder of God's plan.

Our Lady was certainly not expecting the Annunciation, and the whole plan of redemption was most unexpected to humanity—the whole idea of it, that the Father's Divine Son, himself God, should become man, should be incarnated through the agency of this young, unknown girl in a city of which someone was to say, "Can any good come out of that little place?" What was more unexpected? This was the whole plan.

God, speaking through the prophet Jeremiah, says, "I know well the plans I have in mind for you" (Jer 29:11). We don't, but that's wonderful. If we trust a human being very deeply, we would accept that. If you were to say to me, "I just don't get this at all", I would say, "I can't explain it to you now, but take my word for it: it's going to turn out right if you will just do what I'm asking you." And I would venture to say you would believe me. Can we do less for God, who is saying exactly this to us? "I know well the plans I have in mind for you, plans for your welfare, not for woe! Plans to give you a future full of hope. I don't reveal all the details of those plans because I cannot deprive you of faith. I cannot deprive you of hope. I cannot deprive you of the glory of trusting in me. I cannot deprive you of the wonder of seeing my plan as it unfolds. I don't want you to read the whole story and the last page, I want you to keep reading and to enjoy the wonder of what's coming next in the way that children say, 'And then what? And then what?'" God knows the next page, the next chapter, and even the last page. It is a plan, and all we have to do is place our lives at the service of that plan so that without presumption we can say, "Yes, the Word will be made a little less unutterable through the word of each of our lives, a little more manifest because we have placed our lives at the service of his plan."

It is sufficient that God knows this plan. When it is hard to accept things, we should make that part of our prayer. We want to become very intimate with him as the great mystics were in very simple, humble ways, saying, "Dear God, I don't get this at all, but I'm so glad that you do. And I know that you have a plan and I only want to be at the service of your plan." And who of us, in her own life, has not had experience of that? The very things that sometimes seemed so hard, so suffering, so puzzling and bewildering, were the very things out of which would come a wonder that we could never have dreamed of.

In our personal lives there is a wonder unfolding. It is wonderful to keep going forward. Even our Lady did not know the last page. The morning of the Resurrection was not the last page. She still had much work to do with the infant Church, which held together around her, her life still being placed at the service of his plan. Why didn't our Lord take her with him right away? Nor was her life at the service of his plan completed at her own Assumption, because she is still the Mother of the Church. The Church is still living and it will go on until the end of time. And even then her work will not be done, because then it becomes the Church triumphant of which she is still the Queen. And so, let us determine in all the events of each day to place our lives at the service of his plan. This is the happiest way that a person can live.

✤ ✤ ✤ ✤

A Love-Watch

My dear sisters, today we have the heart-shaking Gospel of the Annunciation, when our Lady said her great *fiat*, on which, so to speak, God himself waited. Saint Bernard, in his charming lesson at Matins, becomes quite agitated about this, that she should not go a wrong way. This is no time, he says, for simplicity and for drawing back; he is urging her to say *fiat*. And she did. She said the greatest word that could be spoken to the greatest event in our history, but it was only the first time out of many. She said *fiat* all of her life, not just at the Annunciation. Her *fiat* was not what we would call a "lip service", even though burningly sincere. It was not a matter of words, although that word was great, sublime. It was a matter of going beyond the spoken word to a lived avowal.

At our holy Profession, we said our *fiat*. We spoke a word, and this was sincere. But then it really has to go into doing. This is what our Lady shows us. She tells us not just how to say *fiat*, but how to live it, not only in the large, dramatic occasions of life, but in the little hidden ones. She had many a hidden *fiat* to say in her life.

Her "Be it done" was said over and over and over. She was a very active doer in letting it be done. *Fiat* is a very active word. In the beginning God said, "*Fiat!*" And it was. Oh, was there action! The world came into being. He said, "*Fiat!*" to light, and light was. He spoke that word for each of us: "*Fiat!* Let her be." And she was. I was; you were. In our human *fiat*, we have to be active doers in letting it be done. *Fiat* was not just a lovely word of God. It was a word that galvanized into action, made the light to be, the world to be, the ocean to be, man to be. Our *fiat* must be the action of our whole life, expressed in our giving. Then it really is done; it really is lived.

In one of her antiphons, the Church solemnly tells us that "the fullness of time has come upon us at last". None of us in this room knows when the fullness of time will come for us. God grant we can meet it with courtesy. The fullness of time, in a deep spiritual sense, comes each day, a day which will never be again. Today is the absolute fullness of today. Let us be drawn to love and to give and to spread joy all about us. We are not promised tomorrow, and we cannot do anything much about yesterday, except to regret what was wrong about it. But we have today! We have many hours of this day left in which to love God and to love one another and to spread the joy of Advent and Christmas far and wide, because what we spread in community will not be contained in community. It will spread far and wide.

The Preface of this last week of Advent tells us what God expects: that he will find us watching in prayer. This is where he found our Lady at the Annunciation. This is where he found her at Bethlehem. This is where he found her beneath the Cross. This is where he found her on Resurrection morning. This is where he found her in all the incidents of her life. This is where he found her at the moment of her death: watching in prayer. Will he find us watching in prayer? We hope so, but we must *will* so. We need to ask ourselves some very forthright questions. Does he perhaps find us not watching in prayer but chafing under some circumstance, thrashing about in this situation, this thing that is asked of me, this sacrifice? It is up to us. He wants to find us where he found our Lady, watching in prayer.

Then the Preface says, "Our hearts filled with wonder and praise." Are our hearts filled with the wonder that God is coming to renew the mystery of his Incarnation? Are our hearts filled with wonder over his incredible love? Or are they perhaps partly occupied with other things? If my heart is not filled with wonder, I will always find something to complain about. The more I am watching in prayer, the more I will wonder. There will be more and more to wonder about: that this grace should appear, that God should trust me enough to put this sacrifice in my path. The more I watch in prayer, the more I will wonder. "Our hearts filled with wonder and praise." Praise is the eruption of wonder; it is wonder flowing over, wonder that must express itself. Let this be so much at the center of our thinking, our remembering, our doing, these precious days, that, watching in prayer, we will grow in wonder, our hearts filled with wonder erupting into praise. Peace and a love-watch!

❖ ❖ ❖ ❖

A Welcome Sound

MY DEAREST SISTERS, today we want to dwell on movement, on coming. We have often reflected together on
the great word of Advent: *Veni!* Come!

There is something about the thought of *going* that can
be very sad, very difficult, unless it is completed by *coming*.
This idea of going, left incomplete, we can see as a suffering thing in many ways. For instance, those who are not
yet blessed with the gift of faith, or who have never heard
the Good News, will meet the death of a loved one with
a terrible sense that this person has gone. Death can be a
despairing thing for a family that does not know that the
going forth of death is a coming. But for us who have
faith, death, even with all its tears, and the wrench of
human parting, is a wonderful thing, because death is
really a coming. It is a coming home to God. This is the
whole Christian meaning of death: it is a going forth from
the earthly scene, but only in order to come.

There are many, many examples of how going is completed by coming. Let us look now at just one more: we
all want to go forth from our faults. We would really like
to leave them behind. But we find this something which
in our weakness we easily tire of, something we almost
despair of because it seems we are not going. This is
because we are not focused on coming. Why do we want
to go out of certain things in our lives? Is it so that I can
admire myself for being without these unpleasant things in
me? No, the only thing that gives us the strength to go

from our pride is the coming to a humble Jesus. The only thing that fires me to go forth from my willfulness, my complaining, is the focus on coming, on coming to him who emptied himself for me. When we dwell on this coming to the great Christ of the kenosis who, being in the form of God, emptied himself and took the form of a servant, then we are not so much dwelling on the difficulty of going forth from our pride as on coming to One who has emptied himself for us. If we focus on that, on coming to the emptied One, then we are energized to go forth, and we no longer find anything so alluring in being just full of ourselves, because we are coming toward the emptied One.

Saint Paul said to the Romans that the step of those who bring good news is a welcome sound. In his Incarnation, the Son of God stepped forth, so to speak, from the Godhead. He brought it with him. But in our fumbling human way of trying to express this, we say he came forth from the Godhead to earth. That was the greatest step ever made. This was the most welcome sound heard from the beginning of time or until the end of time, the sound for which the prophets had waited for centuries, as they told the people: "He will come. He will come."

He came into the womb of the Virgin. Oh, what a step that was! In order that he could come, she had to go forth from her own plans, her beautiful plans of holiness. She was going to be so hidden; she was going to be God's little handmaid. Oh, yes!—more than she could ever have dreamed. She was called to go forth from her hidden life, and to come into the fullness of God's plan. When she said yes (*Fiat!* Be it done), one could paraphrase this truly as "Yes, I come." She said, as her Divine Son was to say in his human life now beginning in her, "Behold, I come to do his will."

What did our Lady do after she came forth in response to this greatest announcement that has ever been made, or ever will be made, upon the earth? She came to her cousin Elizabeth. And in order to come, she (as with all of us) had to go. We look at that human scene with a woman's understanding heart and eyes. That was a hard going. She certainly had every need, so to speak, to enter very deeply into the solitude and the hush of that very first Advent. The inspiration of God in her heart told her to go forth from this little place of quiet to a hard, hard journey. That was made possible because she was coming to Elizabeth. All of her life, she was coming. Later at the end of those blessed nine months, she was again not so much going from her little home, the things that were familiar to her, the preparations that her mother's heart had made, as much as coming to Bethlehem to fulfill the will of the Father, to fulfill the prophecy. Later, she did not so much go from Bethlehem as to come to Egypt in order that she might save her Son's human life. Then, she came back to Nazareth. Still later, when she let Jesus leave her to begin his public life, we see her there, briefly, in several points in the Gospel, letting him go, and coming with him: there she is on the edge of the crowd. We see her also in that tremendous coming on the way of the Cross. We see her coming, at its end, to stand beneath the Cross. We see her going back to her little home, empty as never before because his earthly presence was now gone. But she was now coming to make a home for John, and through John, for all of us.

All of these comings of hers were indeed welcome sounds. All our comings are welcome sounds, and we make our spiritual progress possible by the thought of the One to whom we wish to come. This is the whole meaning of going. Whether I go from earth, or I go from a presence, or I go from familiar things, or I go from my faults, which tend to hold me back—all these things are made possible and are made beautiful and inviting because I am coming.

And so, let us enter very deeply into the security of his coming, which makes it possible for us to come to him. When he appeared upon earth, when he came forth, as the Scriptures say, like a Bridegroom from his chamber, when he came forth from the chamber of the womb of the Virgin, there was a welcome—oh! a very welcome—sound. What was it? It was the cry of a little Child. At that time, within the human limitations he had lovingly taken upon himself, this was the only kind of welcome sound he could humanly make. So, that first cry after his human birth was surely the most welcome sound ever heard up to that time upon the earth. Because of that welcome sound, that cry of a little Child, the skies burst apart, the Scriptures tell us. Hosts of angels appeared, singing. The earth (though most of the earth did not know it) was set ablaze with glory, which was to call shepherds to come, which was to call kings to come on a very strange journey. How could they have gone except that they were coming? And how could the shepherds have left their business, their watching their flocks, unless they were coming? They were all answering that first little cry of a Child which announced: "I have come!"

We want to bring in Advent that welcome sound of coming, that bringing of good news. We can only bring this welcome sound to the Church of God, to a world that needs it so much, by making that welcome sound in all the little situations and circumstances that he will indubitably provide for us. We want to come to him in a new patience, a new humility, a new sweetness, a new gentleness, a new love. Let us rejoice in remembering that the little cry of a little Child was the most welcome sound the world had ever heard. So also, the sound of love, the sound of virtue, the sound of anyone coming to God may be a little sound, but it is a welcome sound. And it spreads happiness, joy, hope, throughout all the world. Let us practice today.

❖ ❖ ❖ ❖

Love beyond All Telling

THE PREFACE that the Church reserves for the last week of Advent says that "the Virgin Mother bore him in her womb with love beyond all telling". Surely we all respond to this. Who could describe in words the love of the Virgin Mother for her Divine Child? This is certainly a true and evident meaning, that her love goes beyond all human description. Only God himself, so to speak, could describe the love of the Virgin Mother for the Divine Child. So, in that sense, it is indeed love beyond all telling. In our little measure, our limited measure, we want our love to be beyond all telling. I think part of why we reach out so to this particular Preface is that we want our love to be so great that it can be—in its own measure—beyond description. This is what we want to strive for, these last days of Advent.

There are other levels of understanding of that marvelous phrase: levels that we share with our Lady, and then a final level on which we cannot find her, in which she has no place. After that first consideration of love beyond all telling as being love beyond all description, there is a meaning of love beyond all telling as being the love of doing. I certainly think this is a meaning of the phrase in the Preface—that same meaning that Saint John speaks of in his Letter: "Little children, let us love in deed and in truth and not merely talk about it" (1 Jn 3:18). Our Lady talked very little about it. She said her *Magnificat*; and all the rest (except what was secretly spoken in her heart to her Divine Son) was in doing. Love that is real goes beyond all telling into doing. This is the second level of understanding of that dear and precious phrase: that love beyond all telling is the love of doing. If the love of telling seems to burst the bonds of words, it goes beyond all telling into doing. And so we will want to be very concerned with that, and very particularly in these last days of Advent. There will be many, many opportunities for doing. As the momentum gathers and many things come into the day to claim our time and our attention, far from being an excuse for being less recollected, this is a call to be more so. It is a call for more doing. We can never say, if we truly love, that doing is an obstacle to loving or to prayer; rather, it is the expressed urgency of prayer. Love, when it is real, seizes upon every opportunity for doing. Love beyond all telling *is* love's doing.

Then, I think, there is a third level of consideration, another meaning in this expression: Love beyond all telling is surely love's yearning, love's desiring. The more that love is real, not just saying but doing, the more love yearns and desires to love. We cannot find it bearable that anyone should not be saved, that there should be some who do not know that he ever came. The true lover, the true contemplative, should find this a grief so unbearable that her yearning, her desiring, drives her. "*Caritas Christi urget me*", says the Apostle. "The love of Christ impels me, urges me forward." The contemplative can never rest, so to speak, while there are those who do not know that he has come, or who know of it and do not live as though they knew it.

This is at the heart of our vocation, this reaching out to gather the whole world to our hearts and to suffer the unbearable pain that some do not know he has come. By our very way of living, by our radiance, by our joy, by our prayer and our doing, we show that we know he has come—and we want him to come to everyone. Saint Thérèse of Lisieux said she could not rest in heaven while there was another soul to save. How could she rest? How can *we* rest, and how can we say "enough"?

I think there is one other meaning of that "love beyond all telling"—beyond description in words, beyond telling into doing, and then beyond telling and doing into yearning and desiring. This final meaning is the ache of love, the aching for all the times we have not loved. We have not loved enough to be faithful, we have not loved enough to smile, we have not loved enough to suffer with radiant joy. We look back and we ache over this. It is a very positive ache, an ache that drives us on again. It is the true contrition that bears the temporal punishment due to sin, the temporal punishment due to fault, with a great aching for our infidelities. I think perhaps this is the uttermost meaning of love beyond all telling. It is love's aching that "Love is not loved". Saint Francis wept all night over this thought. But most especially we weep that Love has not been loved by *me* many times. In each infidelity, Love has not been loved by me; in each opportunity unheeded, in each sacrifice neglected, Love has not been loved. There is a great purifying of our love in bearing the ache—certainly not remorsefully (which is just selfishness, more self-absorption), certainly not in anger at ourselves that we have turned in such a poor performance, but in that wondrous ache of the heart which drove the saints into sanctity.

I ask you to take this very deeply into your Advent prayer: our Lady bore him in her womb with love beyond all telling. She loved him throughout his life with love beyond all telling, with love that was always doing, love that was always desiring. And, yes, with love that for others was aching. For I said there was one level of meaning in which she personally has no place—and this is in love's aching. She never had to ache that she had not responded to grace. She had, in truth, to confront before God her immaculate person, her immaculate heart, faithful to grace and without sin: conceived without sin, born without sin, and living without sin. And yet, as the Mother of the Church and the Mother of the recalcitrant, sinful children of all the ages who were given to her motherhood at the foot of the Cross, she knows vicariously the ache. The ache of any mother's heart somehow bursts beyond the vicarious. She does, in some sense, experience in her own heart the ache of all those entrusted to her maternity, sprung from her maternity—although personally, she cannot experience it.

And therefore, we bring, as a gift, our explaining to our Lady what it means to be forgiven. We bring to her in prayer the explanation, as from a daughter to a mother, of what it is like to ache for one's own infidelities, one's own failures. I think she is rejoiced by this. I think her Son is glorified by this.

Let us not take "more to do" as an excuse for impatience but as a challenge and an invitation to love beyond all telling into more doing, more desiring, more aching for past failures. We do not take the increasing momentum of these days of Advent, and their demands, as an excuse for being late, but rather as an invitation to come faster. Let us bear Jesus in our hearts, with love beyond all telling, so that it grows and grows until it cannot be described in words, until it bursts forth beyond telling into doing, and beyond doing into a universal desire and yearning, and beyond that into a purifying and sanctifying and urgent aching.

✧ ✧ ✧ ✧

The Blueprint of Each Day

DURING these final days of Advent, there are two settings of heart that we bring: a sweet hush of the heart and a tremendous eagerness. The one is not complete without the other. The eagerness is made so beautiful, so lovely with the hush of the heart; and the hush of the heart is made so animate, so vibrant with eagerness for him who is to come.

Let us return to the devastatingly simple and all-demanding statement of the oration of the fourth Sunday of Advent, that the Word took flesh when the Virgin Mary placed her life at the service of God's plan. Now, every word is so meaningful: "She *placed* her life." It was not wrested from her by some tremendous gust of omnipotence. God in his omnipotence shows great respect for us. His omnipotence is never a crushing weight upon us; it is always circumscribed by his gift of our free will.

It is such a lovely word, "placed"—so much sweeter, more graceful, than "she *put* it there", or "she *set* it down". She *placed* it. There is such a gentleness about that word; it connotes something that is taken carefully with the hands and set down with great purpose, great intent and understanding. We speak of someone beautifully setting a table: she knows just where to place everything. I remember, when I was a small child, my mother making quite an issue of this, that there is a certain place where you put the knife; and there is a certain place you put the fork, a certain place where you put the cup. I found this very fascinating. I can still see her showing me how we place things, so that everything is right and everything is lovely. It is as though our Lady took her heart, her life, into her two beautiful hands and placed it at the *service* of his plan.

Service, by its nature, is an ongoing thing. And so this was not a single placement when she said to God, through his ministering Angel Gabriel, *Fiat*. This was only the beginning of an ongoing placement, until she finally took her place at the side of her Son in paradise. She was always placing herself at the service of his plan: when she understood what he was doing, when she didn't understand what he was doing; when she could laugh and sing with him when he was small, when she would grieve at his suffering when he was older; when she would break her Immaculate Heart with him on Calvary; when she (and she alone) would keep faith in the Resurrection. She alone really believed him, that he would rise on the third day. He had said so. That was always enough for her. She did not need to understand; she only needed to hear—as she heard Gabriel's message. Her life was in the service of a plan that she did not always understand.

Now, we know that in a material plan we have a blueprint, and we have an architect who draws this blueprint. To the uninitiated, which includes all who are not advanced architects, the blueprint is very hard to understand. Having some experience in reading blueprints for our daughterhouses, I can assure you that it is very challenging to read a blueprint. One must study and study, and always, in a certain measure, one must just believe. But in the mind of the architect, this construction is already standing; it is completed. So, too, in the mind of God, his plan (so beautiful!) for our Lady, for each of us, is complete. But the construction cannot be built without the contractor, and without many to help him. Each of us is the contractor in God's blueprint of our life, just as our Lady was the contractor in hers. This is what we mean by the service of his plan. The contractor may not go a different way.

There have been amusing incidents (and very telling ones) in building projects here and in our daughterhouses. Sometimes the workmen for the contractors grumble a bit. I remember one grumbling quite a bit to me about a particular blueprint of the architect: "They draw these things and we have to do it!" But he knew that he did have to do it, to work hard to achieve that part of the blueprint that the architect had devised. The chief plumber could not say: "I'll do it a different way. There is no reason that pipe has to be laid here; let's put it over there—it will be much easier to do it this way." This would never fulfill the blueprint, because it would not be in the service of the plan.

It is really only the mind of the architect that sees the finished construction. We first receive from an architect a drawing in color, that shows the whole building standing there; and it is lovely. It is a drawing that we can understand, but it does not express all the technique. Then he draws the blueprint by which this will be achieved. It includes all the plans, all the details that will one day make that first drawing stand—not a drawing on paper, but a finished construction, a completed dream.

This is what our Lady did. She laid her life as a contractor of God's blueprint for her. This is exactly what we are asked to do, each in one's own way. God has his own blueprint for the holiness of each of us. In one way or another, do we not (though perhaps not in words) often say the same as the plumber who grumbled, "Why does it have to be that way? There could be an easier way to do this; this is very hard. This takes too much work. I don't understand this. Why is he doing it this way?" May we humble ourselves and smile ruefully that this is often what we do! To have a plan for our holiness—that's lovely. We are all in favor of that; there is nobody who does not want to be holy. And there is no one who will say, "God doesn't know what he is about." But then we really have to obey the blueprint as it unfolds. And it does unfold: there is a foundation, and there is a basement blueprint, and there is the first-floor blueprint. In all of these there are sectioned blueprints. Each one depends on the others. The contractor could come in and say, "I don't like right angles. They are hard on me. I am going to make an arch there." Only, there is something he is introducing that is really destructive of the architect's plan.

There are analogies here with what we are asked to do. We don't have to draw the blueprint, though sometimes we think we would like to. We would like to plan out everything ourselves. And, oh, what a mess we would make of things! In our more lucid moments, we really do know that. Instead, we need to lay our lives at the service of his plan. In our Lady's life, it was not only in that most dramatic moment of all history, when the angel came and proposed God's blueprint, that she gave her answer; but it was every day in the things that—we say it with great reverence, but with truth—humanly didn't make much sense to her sometimes. Yet, her life was never withdrawn from his service. It was always at his service.

Let us go forward now into these final days of Advent with the great faith she had. The contractor has to have complete faith in the architect. If an architect and a contractor cannot work together, one of them has got to be changed. On the spiritual plane, we know we don't want the Architect changed. What we have to do is achieve some changes in the contractor. He and we *have* to work together. I have seen what happened in certain phases of building when the contractor did not work with the architect: there is a mistake in our own monastery where the choir hall is slanted because the contractor did not obey the architect. He thought this was an easier way to do it.

This is really our whole life: to work with God. Our work means only to be at his service—whatever the blueprint of each day unfolds. This is what we must remember most about our Lady: not just that great, initial, super-dramatic moment of the Annunciation; not just the height of lyricism of her visit to Elizabeth and the proclamation of her great poem, the *Magnificat*; not just the travail and, in a certain sense, the ignominy of going to Bethlehem and having no dwelling there. Who would think that this could be part of the Divine blueprint? Yes, there is this shaking miracle, of which the Church's ancient poetry says nature herself staggers back and forth—a virginal Mother! There is a divine lyricism about it. But the cave wasn't really that lyrical; having no place to go was not very lyrical. It didn't seem to be part of any Divine plan. Always, her life was at that service, until her Son's earthly end and then on to her earthly end. After his Ascension, perhaps she more than anyone had to have faith in his little band of followers, the weaknesses of whom she knew better than anyone else but Jesus himself. And she believed that the Church of God, her Son, could be built on these people.

I ask you to ponder this very deeply in your prayer

these final days of Advent: our vocation, which is exactly like our Lady's, to place our life (not to have it wrested from us; not to put it down, but to *place* it) at the service of his plan. This is a daily service—not only the day of our vows, not only the day of their renewal, not at some dramatic moment. Service is a day-in, day-out thing. It isn't a matter of a moment, an hour, a day. Service, of its nature, goes on and on—it is always there. This is what we want to do. This, dearest daughters, is the whole of it.

Let us set out anew to do this, not demanding to know the plan. As I say, even if we could see the blueprint, we wouldn't understand it. But God does. Our Lady was exactly as he dreamed her to be. He has a blueprint for each of us. It is up to each of us that the actual construction, the constructed life, will be exactly what he intended it to be, exactly what he dreamed it to be.

❖ ❖ ❖ ❖

The Kindness and Love of God

DEAR SISTERS, there is so much richness in the Christmas liturgy that we could ponder it for the rest of our lives and never succeed in wresting the whole mystery from it. All I can do, in speaking to you, is to dwell with you on a few of the riches that it offers us.

The Epistle of Midnight Mass tells us that the grace of God appeared, teaching us to reject our old faults, our old impieties, and to live very *temperately, justly, and devoutly* in this world. Now, that is a complete program of life for a Christian. *"Temperately"*—the Church is telling us again and again to rejoice, and then the Church says that we should live *"temperately"*—or, as an older translation put it, *"seriously"*. If we take God very seriously, if we take the mystery of what he came to achieve at Bethlehem very seriously, then we shall be full of joy. If we take our vocation very seriously, then we shall rejoice in the opportunities of sacrifice. Our vocation to the cloister is a call to a sacrificial life; and it wouldn't make any sense at all to answer a call to a sacrificial life and then to be astonished when sacrifice comes, to try to escape from suffering, to try to escape from penance when we came to lead a penitential life. We want to live very seriously, we want to believe in the meaning of our vocation, we want to believe that, when God speaks to us, he always tells the truth. And so taking him very seriously, we cannot be anything but full of joy—he has come to redeem us. Every grace that he gives us is an increase, as it were, of redemption. We are on our way to eternal joy; and if we take these things that he tells us seriously, if we take our vocation, if we take the mystery of the redemption very seriously, then we shall be full of joy. If we do not live seriously, gravely, temperately, if we do not really quite believe these things, if we do not have this burning, serious faith in the value and the worth of everything that we do, of every hidden act of self-abnegation which perhaps no sister in the community dreams of, which perhaps the abbess knows nothing of, then we are not joyful. But if we do believe in the worth and value of these things before God, then we are living seriously and are full of joy.

Let us live *justly*, that is, *uprightly* in complete candor with one another, proceeding always from the assumption that every other sister in this community really does love me, that we are a united and happy community, and that everyone desires my spiritual good. Everyone has her faults, as I am riddled with faults myself, but everyone desires my good—no one in this house wishes me the slightest harm in any way—and so, with such persons, I can live very candidly; I can depend on being understood in the measure that God wants me to be understood. And when I am not understood, I will not be surprised at this because no one is ever completely understood. Certainly, the little Redeemer, the Son of God, was not fully understood, not even by his Mother. We can't hope for anything better, we wouldn't want anything better, but we live justly, candidly, and very simply with one another, never encouraging complications in our dealings with one another. God is simple and we are complicated; and the holier we become, the more simple we become, not the more complex. Let us never make great issues out of small things, never be complex about the very simple mystery of our vocation and our redemption. Both are tremendous mysteries but very simple. Perhaps that is why they are such a mystery to us.

Let us live *devoutly* in this world or, again, as an older translation had it, *lovingly*. Love wants to show itself. Why do we make so much fuss about the so-called commercialism of Christmas? Some of it is wrong—that part which is divorced from spirituality, which is cheap and vulgar and meaningless. But the kind of human commercialism that flows out of the spiritual meaning of Christmas is not wrong. There is nothing odd in the fact that because the Redeemer came in such utter love for our sake, we should want to express this love for him in love for one another. It should be an instinct of the human heart that we should want to give gifts, not only to him, but to one another. This is a way of testifying that we do know that we are "all together" moving toward eternity. We should feel this urge, this very understandable urge, to spread joy to one another, to give love to one another, because these are the only gifts that we have to give.

There is one more thought I want to share with you about what the Second Reading of the Christmas Mass at Dawn puts before us. It says, "The kindness and generous love of God our Savior appeared" (Tit 3:4). This is what must appear in our lives—kindness and love. This is what we are called to give to God by giving it to one another, and we can never give of it too lavishly. The wonderful paradox, the miraculous paradox, is that the more we give kindness and love, the more we have to give. We do not exhaust our small resources; on the contrary, it is only by giving of them that we increase them. The more we are kind and loving to one another, the more we are kind and loving to God, the more kindness and love we have to give. Let this be a kind of escutcheon of our community that, here in this cloister, the Church may be able to say, God may be able to say, that the kindness and love of God have appeared. Let them appear more and more.

Christmas must mean more to us every year, and we must not be afraid of immersing ourselves in its joy. It is the most natural thing in the world that a woman's heart should be moved to tears at the manger, at the sight of that small Person who is the Redeemer of the world, and that this was the way he chose to come, out of all possible ways of coming. He chose this way of sacrifice; his first expression of love was in the context of sacrifice. And he is showing us that it is this way that our love is to be expressed always. Let us hold this before our eyes so that we can show by our way of living that truly here also, in our lives, the kindness and love of God have appeared.

This is the mystery of the Incarnation: that he took on our human nature, and that we are to give back to him what he took from us. In this interchange, this *admirabile commercium*, he came to our level to lift us to his level. So let us dwell on these things, as together we enter into the mystery of Christmas. Let the kindness and love of God appear here, and he will take care that they will radiate out into the world—even as from a most obscure cave they did radiate throughout the world and are meant to be continued in each of us as a new incarnation of his love.